The Inn Way

...to the Peak District

Mark Reid

The complete and unique guide
to a circular walk in the Peak District

(IWP)

InnWay Publications

Published by:
INNWAY PUBLICATIONS
102 LEEDS ROAD
HARROGATE
HG2 8HB

ISBN: 978-1-902001-09-8

www.innway.co.uk

The Inn Way
...to the Peak District

The complete and unique guide to a circular walk in the Peak District

✦

The Inn Way...to the Peak District is an 84-mile (135-km) circular walk divided into six day stages. Detailed maps, route descriptions, fascinating historical quotations, snippets and pieces of information will help guide you through the varied and contrasting Peakland landscape from the wild heather moors of the Dark Peak to the dramatic eastern gritstone edges and the delectable limestone valleys of the White Peak, passing no less than 51 traditional English pubs and leaving you with a deeper knowledge and understanding of the Peak District.

Hayfield

For my son, Ewan

Who finds beauty and wonder everywhere.

Thank you to Rachel Gospel, Ewan Reid, Stewart Reid, Bernadette Reid, Jenny Walters, Tom Bailey, Ian Belcher and Anthony Cake for accompanying me on many of the walks over the last two years.

I am extremely grateful to the following people and organisations who have helped with my research: The National Trust, East Midlands Tourism, English Heritage, English Nature, Peak District National Park Authority, Forestry Commission, Peak Cavern, Chatsworth Estate, Derbyshire County Council and Peak District & Derbyshire Tourism.

I gratefully acknowledge the permission given by the authors and publishers of the books used for quotations throughout this publication. Every effort has been made to trace the copyright holders for these short quotations. Unfortunately in some instances I have been unable to do so and would therefore be grateful for any information that may assist me in contacting these copyright holders. Full credits to author and title have been given within the text as well as in the comprehensive bibliography at the back of this book.

Front cover photograph: Monsal Dale
Back cover photograph: The Great Ridge
© Karen Frenkel
www.karenfrenkel.info

Illustrations © John A. Ives, Dringhouses, York.
www.johanaives.co.uk

Printed and bound by Spectrum Print, Cleethorpes.

This guidebook was researched, written, typeset, printed and bound in England.

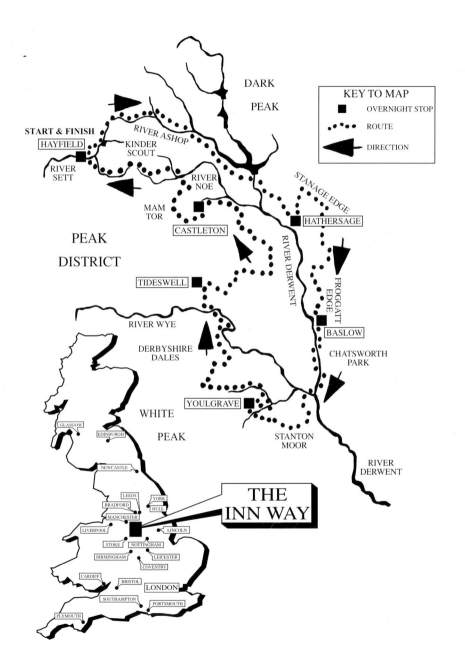

A FOREWORD BY THE DUKE OF DEVONSHIRE CBE

I am naturally delighted to write this foreword for Mark Reid's 'Inn Way to the Peak District'. I am sure that this will be an extremely popular addition to The Inn Way series, which already numbers five titles. The Peak District is one of the most popular places to walk in the British Isles and for very good reason. The landscape is varied, dramatic and peaceful in turn, not far from several vast conurbations and let's not forget the wonderful hospitality that can be found in the many pubs along the way.

I have found Mark Reid's books a fascinating source of local information as well as an inspirational guide for wonderful walking, and his suggested walks in what is now my home patch of the Peak District include so many things that I didn't know about. The route descriptions are sensible, practical and realistic, because the author understands that the main point of walking is to enjoy yourself. He has clearly enjoyed writing about these walks, allowing the rest of us to pick his brains and benefit from his research.

Quite rightly, however, he does not allow us to forget our responsibilities. Although he takes Elvis, his German Shorthaired Pointer, with him wherever he goes, he rightly points out the damage that out of control dogs can do to ground-nesting birds and farm animals; a balanced perspective that is sadly lacking with some dog-owning ramblers.

I am very proud to live in the Peak District, and I am very fortunate to have so many wonderful walks on my doorstep. I hope that this excellent book will encourage more people to explore the Peak District.

Nobody who buys this book will regret it for a moment.

The Duke of Devonshire CBE

CONTENTS

INTRODUCTION

The Peak District stands as one of our treasured landscapes, a region of incredibly contrasting scenery ranging from the wild, brooding moors of the Dark Peak to the delectable limestone valleys of the White Peak, all of which can be found in a relatively compact area. This intense natural beauty draws millions of people to visit each year who come to enjoy the Great Outdoors, breathe in fresh air, relax and unwind.

Long distance walking offers a uniquely different approach to exploring this wonderful area. By spending six days walking through the Peak District you are not only experiencing the geology, landscape, archaeology, history, culture, heritage and weather at a gentle pace but you are making a positive contribution to the upkeep of the National Park. By leaving your car behind and walking for six days from village to village you are putting money directly into the local economy; you have no choice but to eat, drink and stay locally. The National Park is a living landscape and there is a mutual dependence between the landscape, environment, local community and rural economy. It is all inter-linked and the future of this much-loved national park is dependent upon sustainable tourism.

There are also many other benefits to be gained from long distance walking; notably exercise, achievement and a whole new outlook. After the first day, you begin to feel an overwhelming sense of space, freedom and liberation away from the burdens of everyday life. After walking just a mile, you leave everything and everyone behind as you enter a natural world that becomes your own, one which you can savour for the rest of the day. Your only objectives for the day become a lunchtime pub and overnight village a dozen or so miles away, and the only way to get there is on foot. In fact, you start to look at your feet in an entirely new light for they become a means of transport and this new-found pace is a revelation as you have time to discover, absorb and appreciate so much more along your journey. After three days, reaching a busy road or a village is something of a culture shock. And at the end of the journey, your soul has been cleansed and revitalised, your body clock has been finely tuned to a slower pace and you feel, most importantly, relaxed and calm. You have gained new perspectives and new vision. Talk to anyone who has completed a long distance walk and this is what they will tell you.

I firmly believe that it is all about adding much more than you take. By undertaking this walk will you gain nourishment for your soul whilst unwittingly making a positive contribution to the future of the Peak District. You will take only memories and leave only footprints - and you can forget about carbon footprints as the only ones you will leave behind will be muddy ones!

Youlgrave

PLAN OF THE BOOK

The Inn Way...to the Peak District will take six days to complete either as an 84-mile circular walk or broken down into individual linear walks of up to seventeen-and-a-half miles. Each walk has its own section within this book, which is designed to provide all of the necessary information for that day's walk. These individual sections contain an information page, route description, hand-drawn map and a detailed compilation of information concerning places of interest along the way that are brought to life by fascinating short quotations from selected travel authors who have visited the Peak District over the last hundred years or more.

Interpretation of Information and Route Descriptions

Walk Information

Points of interest:	This provides a summary of the highlights of the day's walk.
Distance:	The distance travelled in a day has been broken down into 'morning' and 'afternoon' sections with a total mileage for the day. All distances given are 'map miles' estimated from Ordnance Survey (1:25,000) maps. All distances quoted are in miles and yards, conversions as follows: Yards to metres multiply by 0.9 Miles to kilometres multiply by 1.6 Kilometres to miles multiply by 0.6 Metres to yards multiply by 1.1
Time:	Total time taken to complete the day's walk. This is based upon a walking speed of two-and-a-half miles per hour with consideration for steep ascents, rest stops and viewpoints. This time does not include the obligatory hour lunch break!

Terrain:	Summary of the type of walking surface you will encounter along the way, for example stony tracks, long grass, boggy ground etc, as well as any particularly steep ascents / descents and exposed sections.
Ascents:	Each of the major climbs of the day are listed complete with maximum height gained. This figure is not necessarily the total amount of climbing to be done as most ascents start between 100 and 300 metres above sea level. All height figures are in metres (see conversion table above).
Viewpoints:	A selection of the best viewpoints for each section - remember you camera as well as your binoculars!

Facilities

Inn	See list of 'Public Houses'
B&B	Bed and Breakfast accommodation available in the village.
Shop	At least one shop selling general provisions.
PO	Post Office, many of which sell limited provisions.
Café	Teas and light refreshments available.
Bus	Served by public transport, although services are often seasonal and infrequent.
Train	Served by the Hope Valley Line.
Phone	Public payphone.
Toilets	Public conveniences.
Info	Tourist Information Centres or National Park Information Centres.
YH	Youth Hostel accommodation available in or near the village.
Camp	Campsite in or near the village.

Route Descriptions

The following abbreviations have been used throughout the route descriptions:

SP	Signpost
FP	Footpath
BW	Bridleway
FB	Footbridge
YH	Youth Hostel
Approx	Approximately

Due to the large numbers of visitors who visit the Peak District National Park to enjoy various outdoor pursuits, route finding is relatively easy as most footpaths and bridleways are clearly marked and well trodden. The signposts are often colour-coded as follows: yellow for footpaths, blue for bridleways and red for byways. Often, the path on the ground is clearly defined and easy to follow, however, some sections cross remote terrain and high moorland, in particular Kinder Scout, where route finding may be more difficult, especially in bad weather. Always take up-to-date OS maps with you as well as a GPS or compass.

The route has been walked several times using solely the route descriptions given, however, to ensure ease of use they should be used in conjunction with the hand-drawn maps that appear within the text, with an OS map as back-up. Each route description has been divided into paragraphs that correspond with one of these detailed hand-drawn maps.

RIGHTS OF WAY AND OPEN ACCESS

Rights of Way

Public Rights of Way or Open Access areas must be used during the completion of this walk. The Inn Way only follows footpaths, bridleways, byways, Unclassified County Roads (UCR), country lanes or established paths across Open Access land. On some occasions the path on the ground differs slightly from the Right of Way shown on the OS map. Where this occurs I have followed the path on the ground to avoid creating more paths and consequently more erosion.

The countryside is slowly but constantly evolving and changing; stiles may become bridle-gates, gates may disappear, paths may be re-surfaced, pubs or shops may close. Occasionally, Rights of Way may be altered or diverted to prevent erosion damage or to improve the line of the footpath. Any changes will be clearly signposted and must be followed, and are usually marked on the most up-to-date Ordnance Survey maps. Feedback concerning these changes is always welcome, as this book is updated at reprint.

Open Access

The Countryside and Rights of Way Act 2000 opened up 4,000 square miles of mountain, moor, heath, down and common land throughout England. Walkers can now freely roam across this Open Access land without having to stay on public footpaths. These new rights of access relate to mapped areas of access land that comprise predominantly unenclosed areas of mountains, hills and moorland - not enclosed fields or private land - and are marked on Ordnance Survey maps as areas of yellow shading. On the ground, key access points display a brown circular Open Access symbol as well as local information. Generally, you can get onto Access Land via existing Rights of Way or moorland roads. Farmers and landowners can restrict access rights to their land for 28 days each year, for example during the breeding season. They may also apply for long term restrictions where necessary for land management, safety or fire prevention. Restrictions or closures are shown on the Countryside Access website or on local notices. Walkers using Open Access land have a responsibility to respect and protect the countryside and follow the Countryside Code.

The Inn Way takes advantage of Open Access land across the top of Stanage Edge and on the approach to Win Hill. Sections of the walk also follow existing Rights of Way across Open Access land, in particular across Kinder Scout, along the eastern gritstone edges as well as some of the limestone dales. Always take your Ordnance Survey maps with you so you can take full advantage of this Open Access land.

For further information visit wwww.openaccess.gov.uk

Stanage Edge

THE MAPS

The hand-drawn maps are based upon the Ordnance Survey Explorer (1:25,000) series of maps and are designed to tie in with the route descriptions. The route is easy to follow and is marked by a series of dots along footpaths and bridleways or arrows along roads and tracks (see 'Key to Maps'). Landmarks, places of interest, hills and contours are also given to help you. These maps should guide you safely around *The Inn Way...to the Peak District*; however, they do not show the surrounding countryside in detail. Always take Ordnance Survey Explorer maps (scale 1:25,000) with you on your walks, as well as a compass or GPS.

Ordnance Survey Explorer Map OL1 (1:25,000)
'The Peak District Dark Peak area'. This map covers Hayfield, Kinder Scout, Woodlands Valley, Ladybower Reservoir, Hathersage, Castleton, Mam Tor, Hope Valley and Edale.

Ordnance Survey Explorer Map OL24 (1:25,000)
'The Peak District White Peak area'. This map covers Froggatt Edge, Baslow, Chatsworth, Youlgrave, Lathkill Dale, Monyash, Monsal Dale, Tideswell and Eyam.

Mam Tor

KEY TO MAPS

ROAD

TRACK

A624

– – – – PENNINE WAY – – – – –
OTHER SIGNIFICANT ROUTE

STN
RAILWAY LINE

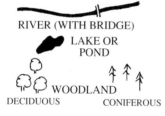

RIVER (WITH BRIDGE)

LAKE OR
POND

WOODLAND
DECIDUOUS   CONIFEROUS

CRAGS OR OUTCROPS

BUILDINGS CHURCH CHAPEL

EARTHWORKS OR
ANCIENT MONUMENTS

300M · 300M
CONTOURS
(HEIGHT IN METRES)

▲   HILL SUMMIT
633M   OR HIGH POINT

YH   YOUTH HOSTEL

CH   CLUB HOUSE

FB   FOOTBRIDGE

P   CAR PARK

PUB 1   SEE "PUBLIC HOUSES"

"THE INN WAY" ROUTE
ALONG PATHS / TRACKS / ROADS

SAFETY

· ·

• Never underestimate the strenuous nature of walking particularly when this is combined with high ground and the elements. Do not attempt to complete a walk that is beyond your skill, experience or level of fitness.

• Obtain a detailed weather forecast before setting out on your walk. If the weather turns bad then turn back the way you have walked. Conditions can change for the worse within minutes reducing visibility and making walking hazardous with cloud, mist, strong winds and rain all year round. The temperature, wind speed and general weather conditions on the high moors can vary significantly from the conditions in sheltered valleys.

• Take Ordnance Survey maps (1:25,000) of the area. It is essential to carry a compass or GPS (Global Positioning System) as some sections of this walk cross remote areas of moorland, in particular Kinder Scout, which are exposed to the elements with few landmarks.

• Your boots are the most important thing; make sure that they are waterproof, comfortable and have good ankle support and sturdy soles. The wrong footwear can mean every step is blisteringly painful - and you will make over 26,000 strides on a 12-mile walk!

• Waterproof and windproof coat and trousers are essential as well as gloves, hat and fleece for warmth; there is no such thing as bad weather only the wrong clothes!

• Travel light as a heavy rucksack can tire you out, cause backache and make your shoulders sore. Take only essential items such as a change of clothes (remember that several thin layers will keep you warmer than thick bulky layers and take up less room), nourishing snack foods, basic first aid kit, blister plasters, hat, sun cream, whistle, water bottle, torch and 'survival' bag. Line your rucksack with a large plastic bag to keep the contents dry.

• Trekking poles are highly recommended as they help take the strain off your knees and ankles, provide balance and stability, help ward off barking farm dogs or inquisitive cows and can be used to test the depth of boggy ground!

• Drink plenty of fluids (not alcohol) and eat food regularly to keep energy levels up.

• Always walk in a group unless you are very experienced and inform someone of your intended route and report your safe arrival. If you are delayed but safe then make sure you let someone know so that the Mountain Rescue Team is not called out. In an emergency summon help with six blasts of your whistle or call the Police (who will contact the Mountain Rescue Team) giving details of the incident and location.

• Take care when crossing rivers or roads and walk in single file (facing oncoming traffic) when walking along country lanes. Do not explore old mine or quarry workings.

• When walking through grassy moorland areas keep a watchful eye for adders, Britain's only poisonous snake. Adders like south-facing slopes and can often be found basking in the sun. Adders will only bite if they are startled or scared - if you are unlucky enough to be bitten seek medical help immediately.

• Above all, keep your hands out of your pockets and look where you are going!

REMEMBER: "An experienced walker knows when to turn back"

COUNTRYSIDE CODE

Consider other people
Showing consideration and respect for other people makes the countryside a pleasant environment for everyone – at home, at work and at leisure.

Enjoy the countryside and respect its life and work
Do not touch crops, machinery or livestock. We have a responsibility to protect our countryside now and for future generations, so make sure you don't harm animals, birds, plants or trees. Wild animals and farm animals can behave unpredictably if you get too close, especially if they're with their young – so give them plenty of space.
Tread gently – discover the beauty of the natural environment and take care not to damage, destroy or remove features such as rocks, plants and trees. They provide homes and food for wildlife, and add to everybody's enjoyment of the countryside.

Leave gates and property as you find them
Please respect the working life of the countryside, as our actions can affect people's livelihoods, our heritage, and the safety and welfare of animals and ourselves. Use stiles and gates to cross fences and walls and close gates behind you. When walking across fields with crops follow the paths wherever possible. Our heritage belongs to all of us – be careful not to disturb ruins and historic sites.

Keep to public Rights of Way or Open Access areas
Footpaths are for walkers; bridleways are for cyclists, horse-riders and walkers. Motorbikes and cars should keep to roads.

Do not make excessive noise
The hills and valleys should be quiet places

Take care on country roads
Face oncoming traffic and walk in single file

Safeguard water supplies

Streams are used by livestock and often feed reservoirs for drinking supplies. Do not foul water supplies.

Guard against risk of fire

Uncontrolled fires can devastate grassy hillsides or moorland, which may never fully recover. Do not start fires or drop matches.

Keep dogs under control

A loose dog can be catastrophic for ground nesting birds, sheep and sometimes the dog itself. Your dog must be under control so that it does not disturb or scare farm animals or wildlife. By law, farmers are entitled to destroy a dog that injures or worries their animals. If a farm animal chases you and your dog, it is safer to let your dog off the lead - don't risk getting hurt by trying to protect it. Clear up after your dog and make sure your dog is wormed regularly.

Take litter home

Litter is dangerous and unsightly.

Safety

Weather can change quickly, are you fully equipped for the hills?
You're responsible for your own safety and for others in your care, so be prepared for the unexpected; follow local advice and signs.
Use up-to-date OS maps.
Part of the appeal of the countryside is that you can get away from it all. You may not see anyone for hours and there are many places without mobile-phone signals, so let someone know where you're going and when you expect to return.

USEFUL INFORMATION

If you are travelling by public transport make sure that you check train and bus times before you set out as these often vary seasonally. Book accommodation in advance as B&Bs and Youth Hostels can get fully booked up during the summer months and may close temporarily during the winter months.

InnWay Publications Website: www.innway.co.uk
A comprehensive site with detailed information to help organise your walk.

Tourist Information Centres & National Park Information Centres:
Bakewell	01629 816589
Buxton	01298 25106
Castleton	01433 620679
Edale	01433 670207
Glossop	01457 855920
Hayfield	01663 746222
Matlock	01629 583388
Upper Derwent Valley	01433 650953

Weather Information: (Weathercall)   09014 722062
Information supplied by the Met Office. Premium Rate calls.

Public Transport:
Public Transport Traveline: 0870 608 2 608
A 'one stop' information line for national, regional and local bus and train services.
Website: www.traveline.org.uk

National Express bookings   08705 808080
Rail Enquiries   08457 484950
There are railway stations at Bamford, Buxton, Edale, Glossop, Hathersage, Hope, and New Mills.

Baggage Courier Service:

Brigantes Baggage Courier   01729 830463
Mr J. M. Schofield
Rookery Cottage
Kirkby Malham
Skipton
BD23 4BX
Website: www.brigantesenglishwalks.com

Organisations:

Peak District National Park Authority   01629 816200
Aldern House
Baslow Road
Bakewell
Derbyshire
DE45 1AE
Website: www. peakdistrict.org

Peak District & Derbyshire Tourism
Website: www.visitpeakdistrict.com

Derbyshire County Council   08456 058 058
County Hall
Matlock
Derbyshire
DE4 3AG
Website: www.derbyshire.gov.uk

The National Trust   01433 670368
High Peak Estate Office
Edale End
Hope Valley
Derbyshire
S33 6RF
Website: www.nationaltrust.org.uk

Campaign for Real Ale CAMRA   01727 867201
230 Hatfield Road
St Albans
Hertfordshire
Website: www.camra.org.uk

Rambler's Association   020 7339 8500
2nd Floor, Camelford House
87 - 90 Albert Embankment
London,
SE17TW
Website: www.ramblers.org.uk

Youth Hostel Association   0870 770 8868
Trevelyan House
Dimple Road
Matlock
Derbyshire
DE4 3YH
Youth Hostels are located at Hathersage, Youlgrave, Tideswell (Ravenstor), Bretton (near Eyam), Castleton and Edale.
Website: www.yha.org.uk

For a detailed accommodation guide send a
Stamped Addressed Envelope to:
InnWay Publications, 102 Leeds Road, Harrogate HG2 8HB.

FACILITIES PROVIDED AT EACH OF THE OVERNIGHT STOPS

Stage One - Hayfield

Hayfield serves as the starting and finishing point because it is easy to get to and has plenty of facilities. Hayfield was also the starting point of the famous Mass Trespass up onto Kinder Scout in April 1932 in protest at the lack of access to the open hills, an event that ultimately led to the National Parks and Access to the Countryside Act 1949, which established this country's national parks, recorded and protected our rights of way and eventually secured access to open hill country. Hayfield is therefore the perfect village to set out on this long distance circular walk through the Peak District.

How to get there:

By public transport - the nearest train station is at either New Mills or Glossop, from where there are frequent bus services straight through to Hayfield.

By car - Hayfield is situated on the A624 midway between Glossop and Chapel-en-le-Frith, in the north-west corner of Derbyshire, close to the borders of Greater Manchester and Cheshire. With limited long term parking available at Hayfield why not make use of the public transport network and save time, money, hassle and the environment!

Facilities - Hayfield is a thriving former mill village on the very edge of the Peak District National Park, with the western escarpment of Kinder Scout towering above. It boasts plenty of facilities including six pubs, several B&Bs, large campsite, restaurants, fish & chip shop, butcher's shop, cafés, general stores, off licence, chemist, Post Office, newsagent, hairdresser's shop, art gallery, Hayfield Countryside Centre (Tourist Information), bus service, car park and toilets.

Stage Two - Hathersage

Hathersage boasts five pubs, a Youth Hostel, B&Bs, café, restaurants, delicatessen, general stores, small supermarket, greengrocers, bakery, outdoor pursuit shops, craft shops, Post Office, chemist, doctor's surgery,

NatWest bank (cashpoint), Royal Bank of Scotland (cashpoint), outdoor swimming pool, toilets, public payphone, car park, garage, bus service and railway station (Hope Valley Line). There is a campsite at North Lees just over a mile to the north of Hathersage.

If you wish, you can reduce the mileage of Stage One by staying at the Yorkshire Bridge Inn (near Bamford) or at Bamford. This will, however, increase the mileage of Stage Two.

Stage Three - Baslow

Baslow offers four pubs, two plush hotels, cafés, a bistro, Italian restaurant, general stores, newsagent, gift and craft shops, public toilets, public payphone, large car park and a regular bus service.

Stage Four - Youlgrave

Youlgrave offers three pubs, B&Bs, Youth Hostel, general stores, delicatessen, butcher's shop, greengrocer, gift shop, Post Office, telephone, toilets, bus service, public payphone, garage and car park.

Stage Five - Tideswell

Tideswell boasts three pubs, several B&Bs, Youth Hostel (Ravenstor), fish & chip shop, cafés, delicatessen, small supermarket, general stores, greengrocers, butchers, newsagent, chemist, Post Office, launderette, art gallery, NatWest bank (cashpoint), craft and gift shops, Library and Information Centre, Public Payphone, bus service and toilets.

Stage Six - Castleton

Castleton offers six pubs, several B&Bs, Youth Hostel, general stores and Post Office, outdoor pursuits shops, gift shops, craft shops, bookshop, restaurants, cafés, fish & chip shop, Castleton Information Centre, bus service, large car park, garage, public payphone, toilets, Peveril Castle and four Show Caves.

All of the above information is for guide purposes only and many facilities are liable to change. ***If it is important - check it.***

PUBLIC HOUSES

The route of The Inn Way...to the Peak District is designed to take in as many of the area's classic country pubs as possible. There is a wide choice of pubs to suit all tastes ranging from village locals to remote wayside inns, haunted pubs, walkers' pubs and a handful of unspoilt country pubs that have remained unchanged for decades. All pubs along the route have been listed - I'll let you make up your own mind as to your favourite ones. If you are relying on a pub for lunchtime food then 'phone to check opening times.

1. *Royal Hotel, Hayfield: 01663 742721*
   Situated next to the village cricket ground and overlooking the River Sett, this attractive three-story building was originally built in 1755 as the vicarage, although it has been known as the Royal Hotel since the 1860s. Inside, several wood-panelled rooms are served by a central bar with open fires and high ceilings.
   ACC / FOOD / FIRE / GDN / TRAD / BAR / INN

2. *Bull's Head, Hayfield: 01663 745511*
   Situated beside the church in the centre of Hayfield, this 18th Century three-storey pub is a traditional 'local' with low beams, tiled floor and an open fire in the front bar and a games room to the rear.
   FOOD / FIRE / TRAD / BAR

3. *George Hotel, Hayfield: 01663 743691*
   Dating back to 1575, this old pub was a Posting House in the 19th Century. Inside, there is a small, cosy bar and snug with low ceilings as well as a separate dining room and lounge with a lovely old cast-iron range.
   ACC / FOOD / FIRE / GDN / TRAD / BAR / INN

4. *Kinder Lodge, Hayfield: 01663 743613*
   Situated on New Mills Road just outside the village centre, this 18th Century weavers' cottage is now a lively locals' pub that has an emphasis on sport with big screen TV, pool table and a good selection of Real Ales.
   ACC / FOOD / GDN / TRAD / BAR

5. *Packhorse, Hayfield: 01663 740074*
    This historic pub stands at the start (or end) of the packhorse trail over the hills to Edale. There has been a pub on this site since the 13th Century, although the present building dates from 1850. It has a traditional yet contemporary feel with a bright, modern interior as well as wood panelling and comfy sofas. Good reputation for food.
    FOOD / FIRE / GDN / TRAD

6. *Sportsman, Kinder Road, Hayfield: 01663 741565*
    This traditional pub is situated just outside Hayfield in the Sett Valley along the route up to Kinder Scout. Inside, there are several rooms including a large lounge with a stone fireplace.
    ACC / FOOD / FIRE / GDN / TRAD / BAR

7. *Snake Pass Inn, Woodlands Valley: 01433 651480*
    This historic inn was built as a staging post along Thomas Telford's famous Turnpike Road so that horses could be changed and travellers refreshed along this tortuous route across the hills. Inside, there is a traditional bar with an open fire. At the time of writing, the pub closes all day Monday & Tuesday - call to check opening times.
    ACC / FOOD / FIRE / GDN / TRAD / BAR / INN

8. *Yorkshire Bridge Inn, Ladybower Reservoir: 01433 651361*
    This large and comfortable pub-cum-hotel is situated just below Ladybower Reservoir dam. Inside, several distinct drinking and dining areas are served by a central bar, with a cosy area around a stone fireplace complete with hanging jugs and traditional bric-a-brac. There is also a conservatory and beer garden. Open all day.
    ACC / FOOD / FIRE / GDN / TRAD / INN

9. *Anglers Rest, Bamford: 01433 651424*
    This ivy-clad gritstone pub was built in 1876. Inside, there is a large open-plan bar and separate dining room.
    FOOD / GDN / TRAD / BAR

10. *Ye Derwent Hotel, Bamford: 01433 651395*
    This imposing gabled hotel boasts a central bar that serves several light and airy rooms with high ceilings and fireplaces.
    ACC / FOOD / GDN / TRAD / BAR

11. Scotsmans Pack, Hathersage: 01433 650253
This lovely pub is set in the historic heart of Hathersage just below the church. It has a traditional atmosphere with plenty of wood panelling, horse brasses and a cosy corner around an attractive fireplace where you can sit in Little John's chair. The pub stands at the foot of several tracks that climb up across the moors, once busy with packhorses as well as travelling tradesmen from Scotland who sold their wares to local farmers.
ACC / FOOD / GDN / TRAD / INN

12. George Hotel, Hathersage: 01433 650436
There has been an inn on this site since at least the 15th Century, originally an alehouse serving the 'jaggers' along the packhorse trails between Castleton and Sheffield. It later became a coaching inn and is now a plush hotel with a large dining room and comfortable bar complete with wooden floors and leather armchairs.
ACC / FOOD / FIRE

13. Little John Inn, Hathersage: 01433 650225
This traditional pub dates back to 1863 when it was known as the Butcher's Arms. It became known as the Station Hotel following the arrival of the railway and changed names again in 1947 to the Little John. Inside, there are several rooms including a dining room, lounge, bar and games room. It is noted for its huge food portions, good range of Real Ales and lively atmosphere.
ACC / FOOD / FIRE / TRAD / BAR

14. Plough Inn, Leadmill Bridge: 01433 650319
Just over half a mile out of Hathersage, this comfortable pub is renowned for the quality of its food. Inside, the bar is cosy with log fires, pewter tankards hanging from the low beams and well-kept beer. There is also a split-level eating area and separate dining room whilst outside is an enclosed courtyard.
ACC / FOOD / FIRE / GDN / TRAD / INN

15. Millstone Country Inn, Hathersage Booths: 01433 650258
This large pub is situated high on the hillside below Millstone Edge overlooking the valley, a mile outside Hathersage along the main

road to Sheffield (bus stop outside). The traditionally furnished bar boasts cosy corners, a stone feature fireplace and an extensive range of locally-brewed Real Ales as well as large windows that give panoramic views.
ACC / FOOD / GDN / TRAD

16. *Fox House Inn, Longshaw: 01433 630374*

The history of this moorland inn stretches back many centuries when a shepherd's hut was built for Nicholas Fox who farmed nearby pastures. It remained with the Fox family until the early 19th Century when the Duke of Rutland acquired the Longshaw Estate. The old shepherd's cottage was then rebuilt and extended to create this fine roadside inn. It is a building of great character with a gabled porch, mullion windows and large chimney stacks whilst inside there are several rooms warmed by open fires.
ACC / FOOD / FIRE / GDN / TRAD / BAR

17. *Grouse Inn, Froggatt Edge: 01433 630423*

There are fine views across the Derwent Valley from the patio of this moorland pub. Inside, the cosy front bar has a lovely stone fireplace with bench seating around the walls and a collection of old banknotes, whilst there is also a back bar and conservatory. It boasts a welcoming 'pubby' atmosphere with good local ales, hearty food and friendly banter.
ACC / FOOD / FIRE / GDN / TRAD / BAR / INN

18. *Devonshire Arms, Baslow: 01246 582551*

This large, comfortable pub overlooks Goose Green in the heart of Nether End. Inside, there are plenty of cosy corners and comfy sofas as well as a food carvery and games room.
ACC / FOOD / GDN / TRAD / BAR

19. *Rowley's Restaurant and Bar, Baslow: 01246 583880*

Formerly the Prince of Wales, this traditional pub underwent a complete transformation during 2006 and is now a contemporary bar/restaurant with a bright, modern interior and an emphasis on good food.
FOOD / FIRE / TRAD

20. *Rutland Arms, Baslow: 01246 582276*

Situated next to the Old Bridge across the River Derwent, this traditional pub boasts a wonderful riverside beer garden. Inside, a central bar serves the separate lounge and games areas, which are warmed by open fires.

ACC / FOOD / FIRE / GDN / TRAD / BAR

21. *Wheatsheaf Hotel, Baslow: 01246 582240*

This attractive three-storey Georgian coaching inn boasts a warm and welcoming interior with a large lounge/bar and restaurant that serves food all day. Cosy corners, traditional décor and comfortable seating add to the ambience. Outside, there is a delightful patio and beer garden.

ACC / FOOD / FIRE / GDN / TRAD

22. *Devonshire Arms, Beeley: 01629 733259*

This classic Peakland pub dates back to the 18th Century and was once a coaching inn that welcomed many famous customers including Charles Dickens and King Edward VII. It is a pub of great character with blazing log fires, oak beams and cosy corners. During 2006, this pub came back under Chatsworth Estate management as part of their exclusive Devonshire Hotels group and, after a major refurbishment, cleverly combines a modern bistro and contemporary bedrooms with a traditional pub.

ACC / FOOD / FIRE / GDN / TRAD / BAR / INN

23. *Grouse & Claret, Rowsley: 01629 733233*

Originally known as the Station Hotel, this large family dining pub once served passengers travelling along the Midland Railway route between London and Manchester via the Derwent and Wye valleys. Inside, the well-appointed lounge has lots of alcoves as well as an open fireplace whilst to the rear is a large beer garden.

ACC / FOOD / FIRE / GDN / TRAD

24. *Peacock, Rowsley: 01629 733518*

This beautiful building dates from 1652 when it was built as a yeoman's house on land leased from the Manners family, Dukes of Rutland, whose crest features a peacock. It has been an inn since the

1820s. Around fifty years ago it was sold by the Manners family but has recently been bought back by Lord Edward Manners of Haddon Hall who has overseen its transformation into a chic hotel. The hotel bar oozes character with exposed stonework and an open fire.
ACC / FOOD / FIRE / GDN / TRAD / INN

25. Flying Childers, Stanton in Peak: 01629 636333
The Flying Childers is named after a famous winning racehorse that belonged to the 4th Duke of Devonshire during the 18th Century. Converted from a row of stone cottages, this wonderful two-roomed village pub remains totally unspoiled with a traditional bar complete with wooden settles, beamed ceiling and coal fire. One of Peakland's classic country pubs.
FOOD / FIRE / GDN / TRAD / BAR / INN

26. Red Lion, Birchover: 01629 650363
The Red Lion dates back to 1680 when it was built as a farm-cum-alehouse on the site of an old farmhouse, although it did not gain an official beer licence until 1722. Inside this ivy-clad pub you will find oak beams, stonework, wooden tables and a traditional 'tap room' complete with wood burning stove where you will also find a well in the floor that is 30-ft deep - thankfully covered by a glass screen!
FOOD / FIRE / GDN / TRAD / BAR / INN

27. Druid Inn, Birchover: 01629 650302
This lovely pub is situated just below the mysterious Rowtor Rocks, hence its name. The building dates back to 1607, although the pub of today is a fusion of traditional and contemporary with two large modern dining rooms as well as a cosy bar and small 'snug' complete with tiled floor and open fire. Good reputation for food.
FOOD / FIRE / GDN / TRAD / BAR

28. Bull's Head Hotel, Youlgrave: 01629 636307
This handsome old coaching inn stands in the heart of Youlgrave; note the arch with a carved bull's head above. Inside, the original layout remains with a cosy bar complete with herringbone floor, separate snug, dining room and lounge warmed by an open fire.
ACC / FOOD / FIRE / GDN / TRAD / BAR

29. *Farmyard Inn, Youlgrave: 01629 636221*

As the name suggests, this was originally a farmhouse although it has been a pub for almost 200 years. Inside, it is warm and welcoming with a narrow lounge complete with low beams and a large stone fireplace at the far end, whilst there is also a cosy tap room and separate upstairs dining room.

ACC / FOOD / FIRE / GDN / TRAD / BAR / INN

30. *George Hotel, Youlgrave: 01629 636292*

Overlooking All Saints Church with benches outside so you can watch the world go by and cars squeeze past each other along the narrow main street. Inside, this traditional pub retains its original layout with high ceilings and several rooms including a traditional bar, lounge and a 'corridor' drinking area.

ACC / FOOD / GDN / TRAD / BAR / INN

31. *Bull's Head, Monyash: 01629 812372*

Overlooking the village green, this attractive stone-built pub dates back to the 17th Century. Inside, you will find plenty of wood panelling and a lovely stone fireplace in the main bar. There is also a separate games room and dining room as well as a particularly cosy side bar.

ACC / FOOD / FIRE / GDN / TRAD / BAR / INN

32. *Cock and Pullet, Sheldon: 01629 814292*

It is hard to believe that this welcoming pub was a derelict barn just over ten years ago. Inside, a large stone fireplace complete with cast-iron hob grate dominates the bar where, on the hour, over twenty-five clocks chime away. Oak beams, exposed stonework, flagstone floor and cosy corners add to the relaxed atmosphere. Open all day.

ACC / FOOD / FIRE / GDN / TRAD / BAR / INN

33. *Stables Bar (Monsal Head Hotel): 01629 640250*

This historic hotel has a commanding position on the brink of the scarp overlooking Monsal Dale. Adjoining the hotel is the Stables Bar, a wonderfully cosy bar that has been converted from the original stabling for the horses that were used to bring passengers up from the station far below in the valley. Warmed by a large open fire,

it still retains its flagged floor and stable partitioning as well as plenty of equestrian bric-a-brac and a superb range of locally brewed ales.
ACC / FOOD / FIRE / GDN / TRAD / BAR / INN

34. *The Star, Tideswell: 01298 872725*
Tucked away along the High Street in the historic heart of Tideswell, this popular locals' pub boasts a lively, traditional atmosphere with several cosy rooms served by a central bar.
ACC / FOOD / TRAD / BAR / INN

35. *George Hotel, Tideswell: 01298 871382*
Situated beside the church, this traditional coaching inn dates back to 1730 and is noted for its attractive stone frontage complete with Venetian windows. Inside, the comfortable lounge is made up of several inter-connecting rooms with lovely stone fireplaces. There is also a separate bar/games room. The hotel is reputedly haunted by a Victorian barmaid known as Old Sarah!
ACC / FOOD / FIRE / GDN / TRAD / BAR

36. *Horse & Jockey, Tideswell: 01298 872211*
This welcoming pub boasts a stone-flagged bar with a lovely cast-iron range, a lounge area with a beamed ceiling and wooden floorboards as well as an upstairs dining room with exposed stonework.
ACC / FOOD / FIRE / GDN / TRAD / BAR

37. *Red Lion, Litton: 01298 871458*
Welcoming village pub of great character overlooking the village green in the heart of Litton; it has been a pub for over 200 years. Inside there are three small inter-connecting rooms that are cosy and warm with a huge fireplace dominating the front room. An authentic Peakland pub.
FOOD / FIRE / GDN / TRAD / BAR / INN

38. *Three Stags Heads, Wardlow Mires: 01298 872268*
This classic country pub has changed little since it was built as a farm and alehouse in the late 17th century. Inside, the rooms are

traditionally furnished with wooden chairs and tables, stone-flagged floors and a huge stone fireplace complete with cast iron range - look out for the petrified cat! The present owners are potters as well as innkeepers. One of the few pubs to be listed on CAMRA's 'National Inventory of Pub Interiors of National Historic Interest'. Open Friday evenings and all day Saturday, Sunday and Bank Holidays.
FOOD / FIRE / TRAD / BAR / INN

39. Bull's Head Inn, Foolow: 01433 630873

This lovely village pub is situated in one of Peakland's most attractive villages. Inside, the atmosphere is warm and welcoming with a wood-panelled dining room and stone-flagged bar (complete with cast-iron stove) from where a few steps lead down to another lounge area. Comfortable pub with friendly service, good food and drink - what more could you want?
ACC / FOOD / FIRE / GDN / TRAD / BAR / INN

40. Miners' Arms, Eyam: 01433 630853

Tucked away off The Square in the heart of the village, this whitewashed pub was built 35 years before the Plague struck and is reputedly haunted by several ghosts! Inside this traditional village pub there is a bar, lounge and dining room with beams and stone fireplaces.
ACC / FOOD / FIRE / GDN / TRAD / BAR

41. Travellers Rest, Brough: 01433 620363

This roadside inn is situated at Brough Lane Head where Brough Lane meets the main road through the Hope Valley. Inside this large family pub there are several rooms served by a central bar with a large stone fireplace, wooden or stone-flagged floors and exposed stonework. Large beer garden.
ACC / FOOD / FIRE / GDN / TRAD / BAR

42. Old Hall, Hope: 01433 620160

This attractive three-storey stone built inn dates back to the 16th Century when it was the seat of the prominent Balguy family. Inside, there is a wood-panelled L-shaped bar.
ACC / FOOD / GDN / TRAD / BAR

43. *Woodroffe Arms, Hope: 01433 620351*

Named after the influential local family who once held the position of the King's Foresters of the Peak. This lively village pub has a traditional bar that is dominated by a large stone fireplace as well as a separate dining room.

ACC / FOOD / FIRE / GDN / TRAD / BAR

There are two more pubs on the outskirts of Hope that are slightly too far off the route to be included.

44. *The George, Castleton: 01433 620238*

This classic Peakland pub has bags of character. The cosy bar boasts a flagstone floor, large stone fireplace and plenty of intimate corners where you can enjoy one of several Real Ales on draught. There is a separate dining room warmed by an open fire.

ACC / FOOD / FIRE / GDN / TRAD / BAR / INN

45. *The Castle, Castleton: 01433 620578*

Inside this historic 17th Century coaching inn there is a warren of rooms each with their own character. The pub oozes atmosphere with lots of cosy corners, low beams, stone-flagged floors, a superb inglenook fireplace and (reputedly) ghosts!

ACC / FOOD / FIRE / GDN / TRAD / BAR / INN

46. *Bull's Head, Castleton: 01433 620256*

Recently refurbished to a high standard, which has given this large pub more of a refined hotel feel rather than a village pub. Inside, the layout is open plan with separate drinking or dining areas including a rather cosy corner with leather armchairs around a large stone fireplace.

ACC / FOOD / FIRE / TRAD

47. *Peaks Inn, Castleton: 01433 620247*

This warm and welcoming pub is situated on the Hope road and is renowned for its good food, well-kept ales and cosy corners complete with leather armchairs where you can warm yourself in front of an open fire. A popular and lively pub, especially at weekends.

ACC / FOOD / FIRE / TRAD / BAR

48. *Ye Olde Nag's Head, Castleton: 01433 620248*

This traditional 17th Century coaching inn boasts a comfortable bar with an original cast-iron Georgian hob-grate fireplace as well as a good selection of Real Ales.

ACC / FOOD / FIRE / TRAD / BAR

49. *Ye Olde Cheshire Cheese, Castleton: 01433 620330*

Walkers and their muddy boots are welcome, as the sign proclaims, in this traditional pub on the edge of Castleton. The building dates back to 1660, although it first became a pub in 1748 when it was known as the Wagon and Horses, later changing its name to the Cheshire Cheese in 1847. Inside you will find low beamed ceilings, lots of rooms and a stone fireplace as well as a noticeable lack of fruit machines or juke boxes - a quiet and civilised pub with a selection of well-kept Real Ales.

ACC / FOOD / TRAD / BAR

50. *Rambler Inn, Edale: 01433 670268*

Surrounded by a large beer garden, this popular hotel boasts several rooms warmed by open fires with wooden, stone or tiled floors and a good selection of Real Ale. Lots of photos of 'old Peakland' line the walls.

ACC / FOOD / FIRE / GDN / TRAD / BAR

51. *Old Nag's Head, Edale: 01433 670291*

Dating back to 1577, this historic pub lies at the heart of Grindsbrook Booth and is the official starting point of the Pennine Way. This walker-friendly pub has plenty of character with several rooms including a traditional 'Hikers' Bar' complete with open fire and a quarry-tiled floor. One of England's most famous walkers' pubs.

ACC / FOOD / FIRE / GDN / TRAD / BAR / INN

KEY

ACC   Accommodation

FOOD   Substantial snacks or meals available lunchtime and evening

FIRE   Open fire (wood or coal)

GDN   Beer garden (includes lawns, patios and outside benches)

TRAD   Cask ales available (Real Ale)

BAR   Traditional public bar area

INN   A classic pub.

Beeley

THE BREWERIES

Great Britain is famed throughout the world for its great ales, with literally hundreds of breweries producing thousands of different beers, each with their own distinctive character, flavour, strength and heritage! Well-loved local breweries play an important role in the strong regional identities of this country, with many producing specific styles of beers to suit local palates. With this in mind, I have only listed independent local or regional breweries whose beers reflect the region in which they are sold, rather than national or international brewers who often concentrate on brand image and profit at the expense of regional identity.

Many pubs and hotels throughout the Peak District, especially in the more rural areas, are free houses, with a handful of tenanted and managed houses in the larger villages and towns. This means that the licensees are free to choose whichever brand he or she likes, however, in reality trade deals and discounts often dictate which products an outlet sells, although the now common 'guest beer' adds variety, all of which means that you may find a whole range of beers on sale that are not listed below. In particular, you will find a selection of beers brewed by independent breweries based in the North of England such as Black Sheep Brewery of Masham, Timothy Taylor of Keighley, Thwaites of Blackburn and Copper Dragon of Skipton who produce excellent ales but are a little too far from the Peak District to warrant a detailed mention below. You may also find Kimberley Ales that were, up until late 2006, brewed by Hardys & Hansons of Kimberley near Nottingham before their brewery and pub estate were bought by Greene King who then closed the Kimberley brewery and transferred production to Bury St Edmunds.

INDEPENDENT REGIONAL BREWERS

Abbeydale Brewery
Aizlewood Road, Sheffield, South Yorkshire

Founded in 1996, this brewery has gone from strength to strength and now supplies over 200 free trade accounts as well as two tied pubs in Sheffield with its large range of cask ales, many of which have unusual ecclesiastical names and striking pump-clips. Their very first outlet was the Three Stags Heads at Wardlow Mires. The brewery is currently expanding with work in progress to double capacity to 150 barrels a week. Moonshine is their best-selling brand and a fine example of a pale ale with a distinctive floral aroma that leads to a crisp citrus taste and bitter sweet finish. *Cask ales include Matins (ABV 3.6%), Brimstone (ABV 3.9%), Moonshine (ABV 4.3%), Absolution (ABV 5.3%), Black Mass (ABV 6.66%!), Last Rites (ABV 11.0%) plus a large range of seasonal ales.*

Bradfield Brewery
Watt House Farm, High Bradfield, South Yorkshire

Situated in South Yorkshire's part of the Peak District, this small family-run brewery was established in 2005 and is located on a working farm. It uses its own supply of water drawn from a borehole to produce a range of award-winning ales, which are all prefixed with the word 'Farmers' to reflect the Gill family's dual roles of farmers and brewers! *Cask ales include Bitter (ABV 3.9%), Blonde (ABV 4.0%), Brown Cow (ABV 4.2%), Stout (ABV 4.5%) and Pale Ale (ABV 5.0%).*

Hydes Brewery
Moss Lane West, Manchester

Established in 1863, Hydes Brewery stands as one of the few remaining regional breweries in England that is still owned and managed as a family business. Based in the heart of Manchester, they own an estate of more than 70 pubs throughout the North West and sell to over 200 Free Trade accounts. In addition to their extensive range of quality Real Ales, they also contract brew cask-conditioned Boddington's Bitter - the famous 'Cream of Manchester' - on behalf of InBev, the global brewer who closed the Strangeways Brewery in 2005 where Boddington's had been brewed since 1778. *Cask ales include Owd Oak (ABV 3.5%), Mild (ABV 3.5%), 1863 (ABV 3.5%), Original Bitter (ABV 3.8%), Jekyll's Gold (ABV 4.3%) plus a range of seasonal 'Craft Ales'.*

Kelham Island Brewery
Alma Street, Sheffield, South Yorkshire

The Kelham Island Brewery is situated in the heart of Sheffield bounded by a mill race and the River Don, hence its name. The brewery was purpose-built in 1990 next to the Fat Cat pub, a famous Real Ale pub that is also the brewery tap. Such was its success that in 1999 the brewery moved almost next door to another purpose-built but larger brewhouse with five times the capacity, leaving the original brewery to become the visitor centre. They produce an impressive range of ales including the renowned Pale Rider, which won the Supreme Champion Beer of Britain award at the CAMRA Great British Beer Festival 2004. *Cask ales include Best Bitter (ABV 3.8%), Kelham Gold (ABV 3.8%), Pride of Sheffield (ABV 4.0%), Easy Rider (ABV 4.3%), Pale Rider (ABV 5.2%) plus a huge range of seasonal ales.*

Leatherbritches Brewery

Bentley Brook Inn, Fenny Bentley, Ashbourne, Derbyshire

Established in 1993 in the former washhouse and coal store at the back of the Bentley Brook Inn, this small but renowned family-run brewery produces a wide range of distinctive ales. The brewery takes its name from the Ale Conner, an official who tested strength and quality of beer to determine the level of tax payable to the Crown many centuries ago. This was long before the days of scientific analysis and so he wore a pair of leather breeches and would sit in some ale poured onto a bench - the stickier the beer, the stronger it was! *Cask ales include Goldings (ABV 3.6%), Ale Conners (ABV 3.7%), Ashbourne Ale (ABV 4.0%), Belter (ABV 4.4%), Belt & Braces (ABV 4.4%), Dovedale (ABV 4.4%), Hairy Helmet (ABV 4.7%), Bentley Brook Bitter (ABV 5.2%) plus seasonal ales.*

Marston's Beer Company

Marston's PLC, Marston's Brewery, Shobnall Road, Burton-on-Trent

Marston's is one of England's great brewers with a heritage dating back to 1834. They still use the famous 'Burton Union' fermenters to produce their Pedigree brand where the beer is fermented in oak barrels that are linked together using pipes and troughs that control the amount of yeast. In 1999 Marston's was bought by Wolverhampton and Dudley Breweries PLC (W&DB), one of the UK's biggest independent brewers and pub operators who renamed themselves Marston's PLC in 2007. W&DB (or more correctly Marston's PLC) also own Park Brewery at Wolverhampton, which produces Banks's Original Ale, and the Jennings Brewery at Cockermouth which they acquired in 2005. The company operates over 2,500 pubs and supply thousands of free trade accounts.

Pedigree is a classic English bitter with a slight sulphurous aroma and pronounced hoppy taste. *Cask ales include Burton Bitter (ABV 3.8%), Pedigree (ABV 4.5%) and Old Empire (ABV 5.7%).*

Peak Ales
The Barn Brewery, Chatsworth, Bakewell, Derbyshire

This small but expanding brewery was founded in 2005 by Robert and Debra Evans in a converted barn on the Chatsworth Estate. Robert, a former school teacher, realised that there was a gap in the market for a micro-brewery in the heart of the Peak District and so established Peak Ales to brew traditional yet individualistic cask beers that would appeal to local people in local pubs. Peak Ales are gaining a loyal following throughout the Peak District. *Cask ales include Swift Nick (ABV 3.8%), Bakewell Best Bitter (ABV 4.2%), Derbyshire Pale Ale (ABV 4.6%) plus seasonal ales.*

Frederic Robinson Ltd
Unicorn Brewery, Stockport, Cheshire

Dating back to 1838, this independent brewery's heartland is the Greater Manchester, Cheshire and North Derbyshire areas although they own a number of outlets in Cumbria due to their acquisition of Hartleys of Ulverston back in 1982. It is still run by the fifth and sixth generations of the Robinson family and boasts an estate of over 400 tied outlets as well as an extensive free trade estate throughout the North West; Robinson's is one of the few remaining large regional brewers still under family control. They brew and market Ward's Best Bitter on behalf of Double Maxim Beer Company who bought a number of brands and recipes following the closure of Ward's Brewery of Sheffield in 1999. They also produce a range of ales under the Hartley's name including Hartley's XB. *Cask ales include Hatters Mild (ABV 3.3%), Old Stockport Bitter (ABV 3.5%), Unicorn Best Bitter (ABV 4.2%), Double Hop Ale (ABV 5.0%), Old Tom (ABV 8.5%) plus seasonal ales.*

Thornbridge Brewery
Thornbridge Hall, Ashford-in-the-Water, Bakewell, Derbyshire

This brewery was founded in 2004 in a converted barn on the Thornbridge Hall estate. Its aim was to produce a range of cask ales that drew on the UK brewing heritage whilst embracing styles and influences from around the world. The result is an extensive range of new and exciting beers including the multi award-winning Jaipur India Pale Ale, a premium pale ale that has a pronounced hoppy flavour combined with a slight honeyed taste and bitter finish. Their beers are supplied to around 70 free trade accounts throughout the Peak District, South Yorkshire and Manchester area as well as a dozen national wholesalers. *Cask ales include Wild Swan (ABV 3.5%), Brother Rabbit (ABV 3.7%), Lord Marples (ABV 4.0%), Blackthorn Ale (ABV 4.4%), Kipling (ABV 5.2%), Jaipur (ABV 5.9%) and Saint Petersburg (ABV 7.7%).*

Whim Ales
Hartington, Nr. Buxton, Derbyshire

This small brewery is housed in outbuildings at Whim Farm just outside Hartington. It was founded in 1993 by Giles Litchfield, who also bought Broughton Brewery in 1995 which is located in the Scottish Borders. Whim Ales is managed by Joe Allsop, who has been the Head Brewer at Whim since the beginning. They produce a large range of award-winning ales including the excellent Hartington Bitter, a golden bitter with a pronounced yet refreshing hop flavour that gives it a floral taste with a hint of spice. Over 30 free trade accounts are supplied throughout the Peak District, Derbyshire, Staffordshire, Cheshire and Nottinghamshire. *Cask ales include Arbor Light (ABV 3.6%), Hartington Bitter (ABV 4.0%), Hartington IPA (ABV 4.5%) plus a range of seasonal ales including a wheat beer called Snow White (ABV 5.0%), a lager-style beer called Kaskade (ABV 4.3%), Magic Mushroom Mild (ABV 3.8%), Stout Jenny (ABV 4.7%) and Black Christmas (ABV 6.5%).*

THE HISTORY OF THE PEAK DISTRICT

It is the diverse and contrasting landscape within such a compact area that draws millions of people to visit the Peak District. Far from being natural, this landscape has been shaped and modified since it was first settled by hunter-gatherers some 10,000 years ago - and this process of gradual change continues. Armed with a little knowledge it is possible to interpret this landscape to discover the legacy of the numerous waves of settlers and invaders who have exploited this landscape over the centuries. This legacy has fused together over thousands of years to form what we see today; the hand of man is everywhere to see.

Following the last Ice Age some 10,000 years ago, Stone Age hunter-gatherers roamed through the valleys and uplands across a pristine landscape of tundra, marsh and woodland. They left few remains, although flints have been found across the Dark Peak moorlands. During the late Stone Age (Neolithic) period some 5,000 years ago, these nomadic people began to raise the first domesticated animals and clear pockets of woodland, especially on the eastern moors and limestone plateau, for pasture and primitive crops. Thus began the process of deforestation that would lead to the formation of the deep peat layer across the Dark Peak moorlands. These people moved with the seasons and lived in temporary settlements. They also used caves throughout the valleys of the White Peak from where they hunted, for example Thor's Cave in the Manifold Valley where excavations have revealed bones dating back to the end of the last Ice Age. A tantalising glimpse of life and death during the Neolithic period can be found in the handful of burial and ritual sites that remain. Some of their burials still exist as chambered tombs that were built on prominent hill-tops throughout the White Peak, such as the Five Wells Chambered Cairn near Chelmorton. The most famous relic of the Stone Age is Arbor Low, which is situated high on the White Peak plateau to the west of Youlgrave. Often referred to as the 'Stonehenge of the North', this spectacular Neolithic site features a circular mound and ditch henge that surrounds a circle of around fifty stones, although these limestone slabs are now all laid flat like Roman numerals on a vast clock face. These Stone Age people also began to carve strange shapes across the gritstone outcrops of the Dark

Peak. The Peak District boasts many fine examples of prehistoric 'rock art' with numerous cup and ring carvings to be found across the gritstone uplands such as Gardom's Edge near Baslow. No-one knows their true meaning - they could be fertility symbols, religious carvings or waymarkers for people travelling through the area.

About 4,000 years ago the stone tools were replaced by more durable metal ones which heralded the onset of the Bronze Age and the dawn of landscape management and more permanent settlements. These peaceful farmers lived in small communities and began to clear the forests, grow crops and raise livestock. Their legacy can be seen throughout the uncultivated moorlands of the Dark Peak where modern farming practices have not obliterated these ancient relics. Here you will find an abundance of burial mounds, field systems, settlements and stone circles. These settlements consisted of a handful of round houses spaced out amongst irregular fields that enclosed livestock and crops, with religious and ceremonial structures nearby, such as stone circles. Stanton Moor near Birchover stands as one of the most important Bronze Age landscapes in England with an abundance of burial mounds, known as tumulus or barrows, as well as the impressive Nine Ladies Stone Circle. Interestingly, the word 'low' is contradictory for it is derived from the Old English word 'hlaw' meaning a hill. Throughout the Peak District 'low' as a place-name or topographical feature is almost always associated with Neolithic or Bronze Age burial sites; there are more than 500 prehistoric burial sites throughout the Peak District.

During the Iron Age, which began some 2,500 years ago, a series of hill-forts were built on prominent hill-tops or ridges overlooking valleys. Despite the fact that Britain had become a tribal society, these were not built solely for defence but were a statement of status and power. They often had religious significance and were also used as centres for meetings and trade. Several hill-forts exist throughout the Peak District but the most famous is Mam Tor, first used in the Bronze Age although its strong defences date from the Iron Age. Away from these hill-forts, the settlement and farming pattern of the Bronze Age continued throughout the Iron Age, although the climate gradually became cooler and wetter which meant that the upland settlements were abandoned in favour of more sheltered valley sites, thus leaving the upland fields to succumb to peat moorland.

Following the invasion of southern Britain in AD43, the victorious Roman Legions pushed northwards arriving in the Peak District in the late AD70s. They soon asserted their authority over the native British tribes and built a network of roads and forts, including the forts at Navio in the Hope Valley and Ardotalia near present-day Glossop. Many of these roads have been incorporated into the modern road and footpath network, as you will find out on Stage One of this walk. The Romans were drawn to this area because of the mineral deposits, predominately lead, throughout the limestone hills and they built Navio fort to defend the valuable lead mines. This Roman military infrastructure was superimposed upon the existing Iron Age farming landscape and culture; the native British people continued to farm much as they had done before although they absorbed some positive aspects of Roman life such as pottery, jewellery and farming techniques.

Following the demise of the Roman Empire, the British Isles entered the Dark Ages. However, this term is a misnomer for this was a period of culture and development that helped shape the Peak District of today, particularly the settlement pattern as well as our everyday language. Waves of Anglian and Saxon invaders settled across the limestone plateau and valleys during the 6th and 7th Centuries. They replaced the ruling British elite and asserted their control over the area. They collectively became known as the Pecsaetne or 'hill dwellers', from where the name of this region is derived - the Peak District. There is evidence to suggest that the Hope Valley remained a British stronghold until the 8th Century when it was absorbed into the burgeoning Anglo-Saxon Kingdom of Mercia. This period was the dawn of Christianity as the ruling aristocracy began to convert from pagan to Christian worship. A number of elaborately carved Saxon crosses can be found in many churchyards throughout the Peak District, with fine examples at Eyam and Hope. A handful of churches were also built during this time in important settlements such as Hope, although only fragments remain.

However, turmoil and change arrived once again in the mid 9th Century when Danish invaders took control of great swathes of Anglo-Saxon

Mercia and Northumbria. This created the Danelaw, where much of northern and central England was controlled by the Vikings. Few Danish place-names survive in the Peak District, which suggests that they stayed away from this area. In the early 10th Century, King Edward of Wessex pushed northwards to beat the Danes in a number of battles and eventually conquer Mercia and Northumbria, bringing them back under Saxon control. In around 920AD he built a fortified 'burh' at Bakewell where the defeated Danish kings signed a treaty which effectively made Edward the first King of England. The vast majority of the Peak District then belonged to the English king, who controlled and administered it through a network of Royal manors including the important Royal Manor of Hope.

The most significant legacy of this Anglo-Saxon period was the change from individual farmsteads to the village settlement pattern we see today. Place-names such as 'ham' meaning village, 'ley' meaning clearing and 'ton' meaning enclosed village or farm indicate Saxon origins. The original layout of these villages can still be seen with their farms and cottages grouped around a small green (for example Foolow and Monyash) or along a single street (Sheldon is a good example) from where strip fields ran back from the houses.

In the late 11th Century things changed even more dramatically with the arrival of the Normans. All land became the property of the new Norman king who redistributed it amongst his knights and noblemen. In the Peak District, he gave vast tracts of land to William Peveril including the former Saxon Manor of Hope, which Peveril turned into a vast hunting preserve that stretched from Tideswell to Glossop. It was governed by strict forest laws and administered from Perverel Castle above Castleton, the only Norman castle to be built in stone in the Peak District. A handful of timber motte and bailey castles were built in strategic places such as Bakewell, Pilsbury and Hope but much of the region was used as a hunting preserve and was quite sparsely populated, so the threat from rebellious barons and marauding Scots was minimal. With relative peace, agriculture flourished during the medieval period with an abundance of villages throughout the Derwent Valley and White Peak plateau. These settlements were often laid out by the lord of the manor to utilise the communal feudal farming system where each villager had arable field strips around the village with open commons beyond where they could graze livestock, quarry stone and collect wood. These settlement and farming patterns originated in pre-Conquest times and continued to flourish throughout the medieval period. Vast tracts of land across the limestone plateau and the Derwent Valley were bequeathed to monasteries based in the nearby Midlands by wealthy landowners who wanted to ensure their passage to heaven. These pastures were grazed by sheep and were controlled through a network of granges or monastic farms. The flower-rich pastures of the limestone valleys can trace their origins back to these monastic sheep walks. Lead mining also flourished, albeit on a small scale, with shallow bell pits following the lead deposits in narrow scars across the landscape known as rakes. Primitive smelting took place across the eastern edges in what were known as boles, utilising the up-draught of the escarpments to keep the hearths roaring. Packhorse routes flourished as trade in goods such as salt, coal, millstones and lead brought people to the area; many of these ancient routes survive today. This trade, industry and agriculture meant that a number of villages developed into thriving market towns such as Monyash and Tideswell. Things began to take a turn for the worse during the 14th Century as climate change, the Black Death and other factors caused a period of economic decline and social unrest. Several villages were completely deserted, such as Conksbury beside the River Lathkill. Farming moved away from arable to livestock and the strip fields gradually became redundant.

The Dissolution of the Monasteries during the 16th Century brought about great change as monastic land was sold off by the Crown to wealthy local families or to sitting tenant farmers. Between the 16th and 18th Centuries the feudal system of open communal fields slowly declined as wealthy landowners created deer parks, such as Chatsworth Park. The medieval strip fields surrounding villages were gradually enclosed by stone walls to define ownership thus 'fossilising' the medieval farming system, whilst the open commons were also encroached upon. New wealth brought a period of house building including North Lees Hall, Chatsworth House and Eyam Hall as well as more humble yeoman farmhouses. Lead mining, and to a lesser extent copper mining, became big business as new technologies meant higher yields and deeper mines. Many of these mines lay on the land of wealthy landowners such as the Cavendish family, which brought them riches that helped fund great building projects. Turnpike roads were also built to replace the old packhorse routes as demand for food and commodities grew from the burgeoning towns. The Enclosure Acts of the 18th and early 19th Centuries changed farming practices as well as the rural landscape, where the remaining open medieval commons were finally divided up into large rectangular fields with arrow-straight walls that had been planned out on maps. In the Dark Peak, the open moorlands were enclosed by walls and were increasingly used by wealthy landowners for grouse shooting.

The lead mining industry had its heyday during the 18th and 19th Centuries when the Peak District was one of the most productive ore-fields in the world, advanced by new technologies that meant deeper shafts drained by steam engines and drainage soughs. Large mines were built such as Magpie Mine, as well as more speculative mines like the ones to be found throughout Lathkill Dale. Other industries gained prominence including quarrying, particularly millstones along the eastern edges, and also a handful of cotton mills along the banks of the Derwent and Wye. The Peak District is home to some of the earliest cotton mills in the world, built during the first throes of the Industrial Revolution in the late 18th Century by Richard Arkwright, the 'Father of the Factory System'. Villages on the periphery of the Peak District, but close to the burgeoning industrial towns and cities, grew into thriving mill towns, for example Hayfield. Tourists began to visit the Peak District, attracted by the spa towns of Buxton and Bakewell but also by the celebrated 'Seven Wonders of the Peak' that had been highlighted in earlier travel writings during the 17th Century.

The 19th Century saw the arrival of the railways that eventually replaced the turnpikes and packhorse routes. The first railway through the Peak District was the Cromford and High Peak Railway that was built in 1830. Others followed including the controversial Midland Railway route through the Derwent and Wye valleys. Initially, these railways were for industrial use to move coal, lead and raw materials but soon brought tourists in ever-greater numbers. The railway network opened up the heart of the Peak District to the 'wage slaves' of Manchester and Sheffield and soon these ordinary working folk began a movement to open up the forbidden hills, which represented the only fresh air and greenery they had access to. However, these hills remained strictly out of bounds, the preserve of gamekeepers and their grouse. This was a legacy of the Enclosure Acts where many landowners enclosed the open moorlands for their own personal use, threatening ancient rights of way and access to the hills. This came to a head in 1932 with the Mass Trespass up onto Kinder Scout, which was the catalyst for change that led to the National Parks and Access to the Countryside Act 1949. Many valleys throughout the Dark Peak were also bought by water companies during the late 19th Century who flooded several of them, especially in Longdendale and the Upper Derwent Valley, with reservoirs to provide drinking water for the towns and cities. Today, there are 55 reservoirs within the Peak District.

The 20th Century brought with it the decline of many of the major industries especially lead mining. However, tourism continued to flourish with more and more people able to travel quickly and easily by car and train to the area; this was their rural 'bolt hole'. There was also a dramatic change in agriculture as farms amalgamated, walls disappeared and traditional farming techniques replaced. Threatened from all corners by urban sprawl, quarrying, tourism and insensitive developments, not to mention the growing pressure for better access to the forbidden hills, the time was right to safeguard and manage this precious landscape. Despite these pressures, the Peak District was still a green oasis of hills and valleys sandwiched between major urban conurbations.

The Peak District National Park was designated in 1951 as Britain's first national park. It covers 555 square miles of diverse countryside ranging from the wild moors of Bleaklow and Black Hill in the north to the limestone valleys of Dovedale and Lathkill Dale in the south. It must be pointed out that it is neither national nor a park; nearly all of the land within its boundaries is privately owned either by individual farmers or large landowners such as water companies, the National Trust or the Chatsworth Estate who then sub-let their farms to tenants; there are around 1,800 farms within the Peak District. The boundary of the Peak District primarily covers Derbyshire, but it also covers large swathes of South and West Yorkshire to the north-east as well as parts of Cheshire, Staffordshire and Greater Manchester to the west.

The National Park Authority is responsible for the management of the park offering advice and assistance to local people and visitors, as well as acting as a planning authority. It has two main purposes:
1. Conserve and enhance the natural beauty, wildlife and cultural heritage of the national Park.
2. Promote opportunities for public enjoyment and understanding of the special qualities of the National Park.

They also have a duty to foster the social and economic wellbeing of local communities.

A very difficult task indeed - it is hard to promote and conserve at the same time! A third of the population of England lives within 60 miles of the Peak District - that's 16 million people. It is one of the most visited national parks in the world with around 22 million day visitors each year, which is quite a burden for the 38,000 residents who live within its boundaries. Tourism is now the mainstay of the economy with visitors spending around £75 million every year, which in turn supports many hundreds of small businesses and jobs.

Within its boundaries are some of the finest stretches of heather moorland in England, a wealth of historic villages, important prehistoric remains, fine stately homes, beautiful valleys, fascinating industrial archaeology and some lovely country pubs. An amazing 35% of the National Park is designated as Sites of Special Scientific Interest by Natural England due to the rare and threatened habitats. Then of course there is the famous Derbyshire Dales National Nature Reserve that covers five of the main limestone valleys. Most people come to the Peak District to walk for it offers unrivalled terrain. After many decades of hard-fought campaigning, the Peak District is now blessed with an extensive Right of Way network with around 2,500 km of footpaths and bridleways as well as large areas of Open Access land that covers a third of the National Park.

The Peak District National Park Authority is now focussing much more on sustainable tourism and development to ensure a viable future for the area. The well-being of the local economy is inter-linked with conservation and public enjoyment. The National Park is a living landscape and there is a mutual dependence between the landscape, environment, local community and rural economy; the only way forward to ensure that this wonderful landscape is preserved and enhanced for future generations is through sustainable development and growth.

By spending six days walking through this diverse landscape, staying overnight in local inns and B&Bs, buying food and provisions en route, taking only memories and leaving only footprints, you are making a positive contribution to the upkeep of the Peak District in a sustainable way. In addition to this, a percentage of the profit from the sale of this book will be donated to local conservation projects within the Peak District National Park.

Baslow

THE GEOLOGY OF THE PEAK DISTRICT

The Peak District is characterised by incredibly contrasting landscapes that draw millions of people each year to marvel at the natural beauty, but what they are looking at is actually the culmination of millions of years of varying influences that have shaped the rocks, which are the foundations of everything we see.

The Peak District is broadly divided into two geological areas: the Dark and White Peak. The White Peak forms the central and southern part of the Peak District and is characterised by a high limestone plateau that is criss-crossed by a myriad of drystone walls where you will find attractive villages and cosy pubs. This plateau is dissected by deep and steep-sided valleys cloaked in ancient woodland through which flow crystal-clear streams. The Dark Peak surrounds this limestone plateau to the west, north and east like a giant inverted horseshoe and is a world of broad valleys, jagged escarpments and windswept moorland. To understand how these hills and valleys were formed we need to look back to the dawn of time when the first rocks were created.

350 million years ago this area was submerged beneath a warm tropical sea that was teeming with life ranging from sharks and fish to minute microbes. Over millions of years, countless sea creatures fell to the bottom of this sea and their calcium carbonate shells were compressed to form a thick layer of limestone. Vast coral reefs surrounded areas of shallower water, which formed slightly harder limestone rock. Today, these ancient coral reefs can be seen as pinnacles, outcrops or isolated hills predominantly around the edges of the White Peak, such as the range of limestone hills to the south of Castleton. The fossilised remains of these sea creatures, in particular the spiral-shaped crinoids or sea lillies, can be seen in outcrops and walls throughout the White Peak.

Around 300 million years ago, great rivers flowed down from massive mountain ranges to the north, now the Scottish and Scandinavian mountains, and then fanned out as vast river deltas across this newly-formed limestone. As these rivers flowed into these deltas, the waters slowed and dropped sand, quartz, silt and mud. Over time, these deposits were compressed to form sedimentary rocks known as sandstones and gritstones. The bedding planes within these rocks can still be seen that mark the action of these rivers. During this geological period, when the river and sea levels were slightly higher, layers of silt and mud were deposited that formed bands of shale amongst the sandstone deposits.

Between 300 and 280 million years ago, these rock layers were pushed up by movements in the earth's plates to form a huge dome, as well as numerous geological faults through which hot mineral-bearing fluids and gases intruded that then cooled to create mineral veins, most notably lead. Around 2 million years ago during the Pleistocene geological period, this dome was exposed to the full forces of nature - wind, rain, ice, sun - as well as the powerful eroding effects of four Ice Ages. During this period of around 2 million years to almost the present day, the ice has advanced and retreated on several occasions, the last retreat being 10,000 years ago. Exposed to such extremes, the gritstone dome has weathered away completely in the central and southern areas of the Peak District exposing the limestone beneath, which has created the White Peak landscape. To the north, east and west the dome has remained and now forms the heather moors of the Dark Peak, characterised by vast areas of moorlands that are drained by small valleys known as cloughs that bring water down from the more resilient moorland plateaux to the shale river valleys. In the east, the boundary of this weathered gritstone dome has created a vast escarpment of sheer edges - including Stanage, Froggatt and Curbar edges - that tower above the shale river valley of the Derwent. Tors of more resistant rock can be found scattered across the high moors and edges of the Dark Peak. These tors rise up as either clusters or isolated outcrops, many of which have been given names. Shales are often found along the boundary between the White and Dark Peak where the soft and friable shales have eroded down to create the sweeping river valleys of the Noe, Derwent and Ashop. Where these shales are inter-bedded with sandstones they create unstable ground that is prone to landslipping, such as Mam Tor.

This landscape has been modified and shaped by glacial ice and meltwaters that have smoothed out the river valleys and carved out the deep gorge-like limestone valleys such as Monsal Dale. These valleys were formed during the end of the last Ice Age when the ground was still frozen and so the meltwaters flowed above ground to create valleys, gorges and waterfalls. Over many thousands of years, water has percolated down through fissures in the limestone bedrock, slowly dissolving it to create underground streams and a vast network of caverns and caves, leaving many of these valleys high and dry. This process of erosion continues; the landscape is constantly evolving and changing.

FAUNA AND FLORA

Due to the varied geology, geography and climate of the Peak District there is an enormous diversity and abundance of plants, flowers, birds, insects and animals. The Peak District stands at the frontier between the uplands of Northern England and the lowland plains and vales of the Midlands, which means that you will often find the southerly or northerly limits of certain plants and animal species such as cloudberry, mossy saxifrage, bellflower, dwarf thistle and mountain hare.

The high moors of the Dark Peak are capped by a thick peat layer, the result of high rainfall, cool conditions and impermeable gritstone that combine to create anaerobic conditions. This process began in Neolithic times when people began to clear the wildwood. By the Iron Age the climate had become cooler and so these upland fields were abandoned and the pastures slowly developed a layer of peat. Pockets of ancient oak and birch woodland can still be found in some of the more secluded cloughs that border the high moorland hills. The high moors are now bereft of trees but the landscape and eco-system of this peat moorland is of international importance due to its rarity. It may not support a diverse range of species but it is a special landscape where rare plants and animals have developed over thousands of years to cope with the harsh conditions and poor nutrients. On wet and damp areas of moorland you will find plants such as sphagnum moss, the key ingredient of peat formation, as well as bog asphodel, common butterwort, cotton grass and the rare insect-eating sundew. On better-drained moorland you will find a carpet of heather (common ling, cross-leaved and bell), bracken and bilberry. For a few weeks a year during late summer these heather moors come to life when millions of tiny purple flowers come into bloom. The peat and heather moors are fragile and prone to erosion due to pollution, over-grazing and too many boots. On the highest and most exposed parts the vegetation cover has eroded away completely leaving the peat exposed to the elements, thus causing it to wash away. Steps are being taken to arrest this problem by re-seeding areas and damming some of the natural drainage channels to prevent run-off. This open moorland is of international importance for ground-nesting birds such as curlew, lapwing, golden plover and the ubiquitous red grouse. In fact, the heather moors are managed for the benefit of the grouse by rotational burning that creates a patchwork of young shoots and older plants for the grouse to feed on and nest in. This ensures that enough red grouse are reared for the Glorious Twelfth of August when the grouse shooting season begins. A number of birds of prey can often be seen across these moorlands as well as the wooded cloughs including the short-eared owl, peregrine falcon, kestrel and merlin. Other smaller birds may be seen on the moorland fringes and in the cloughs such as skylark, meadow pipit and wheatear. On south-facing slopes you may catch a glimpse of an adder, Britain's only poisonous snake, slow-worm or common lizard, whilst across the moors you will find rabbit, weasel, stoat, fox, mice, voles, shrews and the only population of mountain hare in England.

The wide river valleys of the Derwent, Noe and Ashop have relatively fertile soils that support mixed woodland and grazing pastures, with the occasional wild flower meadow. Many of these valleys have been flooded to slake the thirst of the surrounding cities. Not only are these reservoirs important for water supply and recreation, they also support a surprising amount of wildlife particularly in the coniferous forests that cloak the valley sides including birds such as goshawk, tawny owl, sparrowhawk, redstart, goldcrest and siskin. Further down the Derwent Valley you will find the much more managed landscape of Chatsworth Park where deer roam and where you may also spot a squirrel, badger or fox.

The White Peak plateau is a landscape of green fields dissected by drystone walls that are predominantly used for livestock grazing as the thin alkaline soils are not suitable for arable farming. Traditional hay meadows were once a common sight across the plateau, a sea of colour in early summer with up to fifty different grasses and meadow flowers in a single field. A number of meadows still exist where you will find clover, buttercup, ribwort, hay rattle, ox-eye daisy, forget-me-not, common knapweed, cowslip and lady's bedstraw to name but a few as well as marsh marigold and meadowsweet in damper areas beside streams. These meadows attract brown hare, curlew, lapwing and skylark, whose soaring song is one of the joys of spring.

The jewel in the 'wildlife' crown are the limestone valleys, renowned for their abundant fauna and flora due to the combination of steep valley sides, scree slopes, grasslands, scrub, woodland and rivers. Many of these valleys are protected as National Nature Reserves. Throughout these valleys there are pockets of ancient ash woodland that once covered the White Peak, for example Meadow Place Wood in Lathkill Dale, saved from the axe due to the steep slopes. These areas of woodland have developed over many centuries and support a mixture of trees, shrubs, undergrowth, plants and flowers with an amazing variety of species; in Cressbrook Dale over fifty plant species have been recorded in one square metre! Beneath the canopy of ash, birch, hazel and hawthorn you will find many woodland plants such as lily of the valley, wood anemone, ransom (wild garlic), dog's mercury, great willow herb, yellow archangel, hart's tongue fern, mezereon, primrose and bluebell. Where the tree cover is more scattered will also find common dog violet, bloody cranesbill, ragged robin, foxglove, lady's smock, red campion, herb paris and meadowsweet. In the upper reaches of these valleys where sweeping swards of close-cropped grass carpet the slopes you will find a glorious spring display of early purple orchid, cowslip, mountain pansy, wild thyme, common rock rose, great mullein, lesser meadow rue, bird's foot trefoil, dwarf thistle and Jacob's ladder. The old lead mine workings are often colonised by spring sandwort, also known as leadwort, which can survive the toxic conditions. The White Peak rivers are amongst the purest in England due to the limestone bedrock and support watercress, crowfoot and the Derbyshire feather-moss whilst in the water you may spot water vole, otter, white-clawed crayfish, trout, bullhead and brook lamprey. Along the wooded riverbanks you may see kingfisher, spotted flycatcher, dipper, sedge warbler, grey wagtail, stonechat, pied wagtail, housemartin, swallow, swift, grey heron, moorhen, coot, and grebe as well as various dragonflies and butterflies. Amongst the trees you may catch a glimpse of willow warbler, treecreeper, woodwarbler, stonechat, mistle thrush, wren, great tit, coal tit, bullfinch, goldfinch, great spotted and green woodpecker whilst at dusk barn owl, pipistrelle and long-eared bat may be seen darting across wooded fields and valleys.

Eyam

STAGE ONE

. . . .

HAYFIELD
to
HATHERSAGE

✦

"I followed the historic Snake Path up out of Hayfield, walking in the footsteps of those famous trespassers. The heather and bracken had just started to show the tan tones of autumn and there was a noticeable bite to the air. There was time to rest and admire the view across Kinder Reservoir towards the shattered scarp towering above. Thoughts began to drift back to the 1930s and a time of nailed boots and tweed jackets when trespass signs littered the countryside and a relaxing day on the hills was so often marred by an ugly exchange with a gun-toting gamekeeper. The only thing I was toting was a trekking pole. I made my way up through the dramatic ravine of William Clough then down alongside the infant River Ashop, taking in the starkly beautiful landscape as I followed the sinuous path through sodden peat and across steep clough-sides until I reached the Snake Pass Inn. What possible harm could they have done to warrant being imprisoned for walking across the open hills? But their sacrifice is my freedom."

Mark Reid
September 2005

WALK INFORMATION

Points of interest:	In the footsteps of the Mass Trespass, dramatic ravines, wild moorland, the source of the River Ashop, an historic coaching inn, marching along the Roman road, a moorland waymarker that offers hope, legionary ghosts, the Dark Peak's finest viewpoint and a bridge across the counties.

Distance:

Hayfield to Snake Pass	6.5 miles
Snake Pass to Yorkshire Bridge	7.5 miles
Yorkshire Bridge to Hathersage	3.5 miles
Total	17.5 miles

Time: Allow 8 hours

Terrain: From Hayfield, our route follows the Snake Path all the way to the Snake Pass (A57). At first, this is a clear track/path that climbs up across Middle Moor before skirting above Kinder Reservoir (steep drops) to reach the foot of William Clough. A path then heads up through this ravine, crossing and re-crossing the stream (rough in places) with a final steep climb up a stone-pitched path to reach Ashop Head. A clear path then leads steadily down alongside the infant River Ashop, crossing side-streams and boggy ground. The valley gradually becomes more pronounced (Ashop Clough) and the path traverses the steep valley side (steep drops) to reach the Snake Pass. From the Snake Pass, a grassy path heads down through the Woodlands Valley to reach Alport Bridge from where a rough stony track climbs steeply up across the eastern flanks of Kinder Scout to reach Hope Cross. The track continues up to the summit of Win Hill (rocky outcrops - exposed to the elements). The descent from Win Hill to Yorkshire Bridge is steep and rocky through a wooded ravine (Parkin Clough). From Yorkshire Bridge, field paths and country lanes lead to Hathersage.

The section from Kinder Reservoir to the Snake Pass heads across remote moorland with rough, boggy ground and steep drops to the side of the path in places. Navigation may be difficult in poor weather - take OS maps and compass. This walk includes several steep sections and fords numerous streams which may be difficult after rain. Take care crossing the A57 and A6013.

Open Access land: The track from SK165 868 (near Hope Cross) to the summit of Win Hill via Wooler Knoll and Hope Brink is a permissive path across Open Access Land. See local signs for information or visit www.openaccess.gov.uk. This is the most direct route to Win Hill, although there are Rights of Way that lead less directly to the summit. If this permissive path is no longer available, refer to OS Explorer OL1 and follow the Rights of Way.

Ascents:

Ashop Head	510 metres
Hope Cross	320 metres
Win Hill	463 metres

Viewpoints

Snake Path overlooking Kinder Reservoir from White Brow.

Far-reaching views from the Snake Path as it heads down through Ashop Clough.

Views from the Roman Road as it traverses Cowms Moor.

The Roman Road climbing up from Alport

Bridge looking back across the Woodlands Valley.
Vale of Edale from Hope Cross.
The summit of Win Hill.

FACILITIES

. . . .

Hayfield	Inn / B&B / Shop / PO / Café / Bus / Phone / Toilets / Info / Camp
Snake Pass	Inn / Phone / Bus
Yorkshire Bridge	Inn / Phone / Bus
Bamford	Inn / B&B / Shop / PO / Bus / Train / Phone / Toilets / Camp
Hathersage	Inn / B&B / Shop / PO / Café / Bus / Train / Phone / Toilets / YH

ROUTE DESCRIPTION

. . . .

(Map One)

From the bridge across the River Sett in the centre of Hayfield, follow the main road across the bridge (away from St Matthew's Church) passing the Royal Hotel across to your right then take the first turning to the right along Bank Street that quickly leads up to join Kinder Road. Turn right along Kinder Road and follow this gently rising up through the village, curving to the left then gently to the right then, where the road levels out and the houses end on your right, take the lane up to the left (SP 'Snake Inn via William Clough & Ashop Valley'). Where this lane forks after a short distance, follow the left-hand enclosed track climbing up and bending up to the right to reach a kissing-gate beside a gate across the track. Head through the gate and follow the track climbing steadily up to soon reach another gate across the track, after which carry on along the stony track alongside the wall on your left up to reach another kissing-gate in a wall across your path (Twenty Trees just ahead). After the kissing-gate, carry straight on along the clear path rising up (passing Twenty Trees to your left) to reach another kissing-gate in the top corner of the field. After this kissing-gate, turn left alongside the wall on your left then, after approx. 100 yards, the path gradually bears away from the wall heading up across the field to reach another kissing-gate beside a gate in the wall across your path (three-quarters of the way up the field). After this gate, head straight on along the wide path alongside the wall on your left then, where this wall bends sharply away, carry straight on along the track and follow it as it sweeps round to the right to reach a kissing-gate beside a gate in a wall (white Shooting Cabin ahead). Head through the gate (National Trust sign 'Snake Path') and follow the wide path straight on alongside the wall at first then across heather moorland towards the Shooting Cabin. As you approach the Shooting Cabin you reach a junction of paths (SP) where you follow the rough but clear path that branches off to the right (do not head up to the Shooting Cabin) then, where this path forks after a short distance (SP), take the right-hand path and follow it curving round to the left (Kinder Reservoir comes into view) gradually dropping down to join a wall on your right. Follow the path straight on alongside this wall (SP 'To the Snake Inn') heading across the hillside (White Brow) with Kinder Reservoir down to your right then, where this wall/fence bends down to the right and the path forks (head of reservoir down to your right), carry straight on along the narrow path (ignore path down to right). Follow this path straight on across the steep hillside and down to reach the stream at the foot of the deep ravine of William Clough.

Cross the stream and follow the clear but narrow path heading up through William Clough, crossing and re-crossing the stream and passing several waterfalls climbing steadily up to reach an obvious fork in the valley after just over 0.5 miles. Follow the right-hand fork climbing steadily up through the upper reaches of William Clough to soon reach the head of the valley where a stone-pitched path leads steeply up out of William Clough. A broad, stony path then continues straight on gently rising up (ignore flagged path off to right) to reach the 'crossroads' of paths at the top of the pass (Ashop Head) where the Pennine Way cuts across the Snake Path (waymarker post), with the Kinder Scout plateau up to your right.

At this 'crossroads' of paths, head straight on (waymarker 'Snake Inn') along a clear path, which soon becomes paved with flagstones and leads on for about 400 yards to reach a ford across a small stream (source of the River Ashop). After this stream, carry straight on along the clear path (flagged path soon disappears) heading down alongside the infant River Ashop on your right set in a shallow valley. The path soon drops down onto the floor of this shallow valley where you carry straight on heading downstream fording the infant river several times across rough boggy ground. Beyond this rough section, the clear narrow path continues straight on heading down through the valley alongside the River Ashop on your right for just over 1.5 miles crossing several side-streams, with the valley gradually becoming wider and deeper (northern rim of Kinder Scout towering above), to eventually reach a ruinous stone barn and FB across the river just down to your right. Do not head down to this barn/FB but carry straight on along the narrow path across the steep hillside of Ashop Clough, with the river down to your right, for a further 0.75 miles to reach a stile that leads into Snake Plantation. Cross the stile and follow the path straight on through the forest then, as you near the end of the forest, ignore the steps up to the left and carry straight on to quickly reach a stile over a fence at the end of the forest. Cross the stile and carry straight on to join the banks of the River Ashop (waterfalls), which you follow downstream alongside the edge of the forest on your left then follow this forest-edge curving round to the left to quickly reach a FB across Lady Clough (side-stream). Cross the FB then turn immediately right (ignore bridlegate) alongside the fence/forest on your left (Lady Clough on your right) to soon reach a bridlegate, after which follow the path climbing up through the forest to reach the A57 Snake Pass *(caution – fast road). Snake Pass Inn short detour to right along A57.*

As you reach the A57 (Snake Pass), cross the road *(take care)* and take the track opposite to the left through a bridle-gate beside a double gate (SP 'Alport Bridge'), after which follow the track to the right climbing up through the forest for 350 yards then, where it forks, follow the left-hand track climbing up to quickly reach a clear, level footpath across your path. Turn right along this path to soon reach a stile that leads out onto Alport Moor (National Trust sign 'Alport Moor'). *This track up through the forest is a permissive path across Open Access Land. If this permissive path is no longer available, head up along the A57 for 0.25 miles then take the FP to the right (SP 'Alport Bridge via Old Roman Road and Oyster Clough') and follow this path through the forest for almost 0.5 miles to reach the stile that leads out onto Alport Moor.*

(Map Three)

Cross the stile (National Trust sign 'Alport Moor') and follow the path (Roman Road) straight on climbing gently up across the grassy moorland then, where the path forks after approx. 100 yards, follow the right-hand path straight on to re-join the forest on your right. Head straight on alongside this forest then, where the forest ends, follow the path alongside the wall on your right sweeping round to the left steeply down into the ravine of Oyster Clough to reach a ford across the stream. Cross the stream and follow the wall as it bends sharply round to the right up to a gate (sheep-pens to your left). After the gate, carry straight on alongside the wall on your right (Kinder Scout across to your right) to soon reach a stile beside a gate in a fence across your path (just beyond a stream). After the gate, follow the grassy path straight on bearing very slightly to the left across the grassy hillside (leaving the wall to bend down to the right) then follow the path as it bends round to the left following the curve of the hillside (Upper House Farm down to your right) to reach a stile over a fence. Cross the stile and carry straight on across the field bearing very slightly to the right to join the wall on your right - follow the clear path straight on alongside this wall across several rough fields (Cowms Moor) heading down through the Woodlands Valley for 1 mile (keep to the wall all the way) to reach the buildings of Hayridge Farm.

As you approach the gate that leads into the farmyard, bear left up the field to a ladder stile beside a bridle-gate (above the farm buildings), after which head straight on across the field to join a stony track to your right just beyond the farm buildings. Follow this track straight on (away from the farm) for a short distance then, where the fence bends sharply down to the right, turn right off this track (SP) down to reach a stile over a fence. After the stile, head down (River Alport down to your left) to soon reach a wall-stile, after which follow the path to the right to reach the A57 beside Alport Bridge. Cross the road *(take care)* and take the track directly opposite (SP 'To Hope & Edale') through a gate and down to reach a ford/FB across the River Ashop just below some concrete water sluices. After the ford you come to a crossroads of tracks where you follow the track ahead curving round to the left then round to the right and gradually climbing up (River Ashop across to your left) to reach a fork in the track just below Upper Ashop Farm. Carry straight on down over a ford across a stream then up to a ladder stile beside a gate (National Trust sign 'Blackley Hey'), after which follow the track up to join a metalled lane. Turn left along this lane then, where it bends down to the left after 250 yards, take the stony track branching off up to the right (SP 'Hope Cross'). Follow this track climbing steeply up out of the Woodlands Valley. The track levels out after just over 0.5 miles - continue along this track and follow it round over a ford across Blackley Clough then across the lower eastern flanks of Kinder Scout for a further 0.5 miles alongside a wall on your left (keep to the track all the way) gently dropping down to reach a 'crossroads' of paths and tracks (wall ends on your left). Head straight on through the gate and follow the track gently dropping down to reach another gate in a wall beside Hope Cross (forest on your left).

(Map Four)

Head through the gate passing Hope Cross on your left and follow the sandy/stony track straight on across the ridge alongside the forest on your left at first then gradually bearing away down to reach a gate in a wall across the track. Just after the gate the track forks, take the left-hand track and follow this rising steadily up to re-join the forest/tumbledown wall on your left. Head along the track rising gently up alongside this forest/wall then, where the track levels out (as it heads across Wooler Knoll) bear very slightly to the right away from the forest (still heading along track) to reach a large gap in a tumbledown wall (solitary stone gatepost). After the wall-gap, follow the wide path straight on heading steadily up for 1.5 miles to reach the summit of Win Hill. Follow the path across the summit outcrops then quite steeply down (stone-pitched path) to reach a stile in a wall, after which follow the path straight down the hillside (stone-pitched path for most of the way) then down through woodland to soon reach an enclosed track across your path and a junction of paths. Head straight on through the small gate (SP 'Yorkshire Bridge') just after which the path forks, follow the clearer path to the right heading steeply down through woodland alongside a stream on your right to soon reach a grassy track across your path. Carry straight on along the rocky path heading very steeply down through Parkin Clough alongside the stream (take care) for almost 0.5 miles to reach a clear track across your path. Cross the track and head straight down some steps to quickly join a metalled lane just above the River Derwent, where you turn right to reach Yorkshire Bridge across the Derwent.

Cross Yorkshire Bridge and follow the road up to reach the main A6013 road. Turn left along the main road then, after a few paces, take the turning to the right along New Road *(Yorkshire Bridge Inn just ahead along A6013)*. Follow this road climbing up passing Mooredge House on your right after 0.25 miles, after which continue up along the road for a further 200 yards gently curving to the left then take the driveway off to the right and cross the stile immediately to the right that leads out onto a field (SP) - *do not follow the driveway towards the house*. After the stile, head left down across the field to reach a small gate in the bottom corner then over a wall-stile just to your right, after which head straight down the field keeping close to the fence on your left to reach a squeeze-stile in the bottom corner. After the squeeze-stile, turn left alongside the fence/wall on your left to reach a tumbledown wall across your path (old well on your left), after which gradually bear right across the field to reach a small gate in the hedge to your right beside the houses on the edge of Bamford (ignore stile in field corner ahead). Follow the enclosed path down between the houses to reach the main road through Bamford.

(Map Five)

Turn left along the main road into the centre of the village then, where the road bends to the right, take the turning to the left passing in front of the Anglers' Rest. Follow this road (Taggs Knoll) straight on to soon reach a crossroads where you carry straight on along Joan Lane climbing up then, where this lane forks, follow the right-hand lane heading down out of Bamford. After you have left the houses behind, continue along this lane for a further 0.25 miles to reach a crossroads beside the entrance gates to Bamford Water Treatment Works. Head straight on along Hurstclough Lane and then where this lane forks after 150 yards take the right-hand lane and follow this through woodland (golf course to your right) then down into the wooded valley of Hurst Clough. Just after the road crosses the stream at the bottom of Hurst Clough take the FP to the right up some steps and through a small gate (SP). Follow the path climbing steeply up to soon reach a squeeze-stile in a tumbledown wall at the top of the wooded bank, after which carry straight on (waymarker) gently rising up across three fields (keeping close to the field boundary on your left) to reach a small gate that leads back onto Hurstclough Lane (SP). Turn right along the lane for a short distance then, where it bends sharp left, take the BW to the right on this bend through a bridle-gate (SP). Follow the enclosed grassy path straight on gently dropping down to join a clear track that quickly leads down to reach a crossroads of tracks beside the entrance to Nether Hurst Farm. Carry straight on along the track to soon reach a T-junction just beyond the farmhouse where you cross the stile beside the gate ahead (do not head along the tracks). After the stile, turn right alongside the hedge on your right down to reach a FB across a stream, after which walk straight on climbing up the field (paved trod) alongside the field boundary on your right to reach a field-gate on your right (track bends away to the right) where you carry straight on up the paved trod to quickly reach another (smaller) gate to your right. Head through the gate and follow the grassy path straight on gently rising up alongside a line of trees on your left and follow this curving to the left up to reach a bridle-gate in a wall/hedge that leads onto a road (SP). Turn right down along this road then, at the road junction, follow the road bending to the right towards 'Hathersage' (Coggers Lane). Follow this road down for approx. 0.25 miles then, where Hathersage comes into view, take the FP to the left (SP) over a wall-stile. After the stile, head to the right down across the field, through an old hedge-line then down to reach a stile in the far bottom corner after which cross another stile immediately to your left at the bottom of the enclosed path. After the stile, head straight down the hillside, over a metalled lane to reach a FB across Hood Beck. After the FB, turn right along the streamside path across fields then skirting the gardens of a house and the cricket pitch (keep to streamside) to reach the houses on the outskirts of Hathersage. Carry on along the streamside path into the centre of Hathersage.

Hayfield

MAP ONE

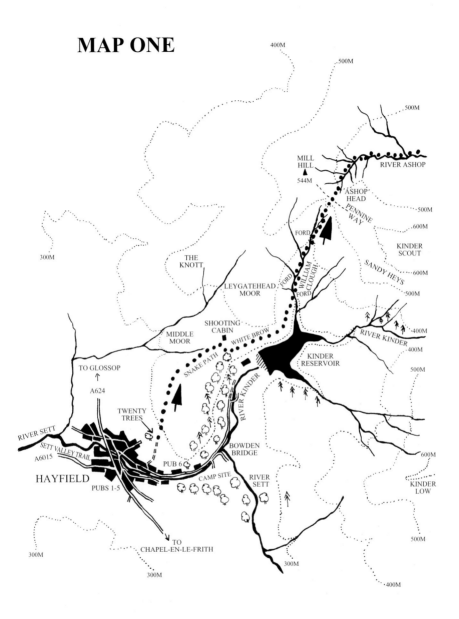

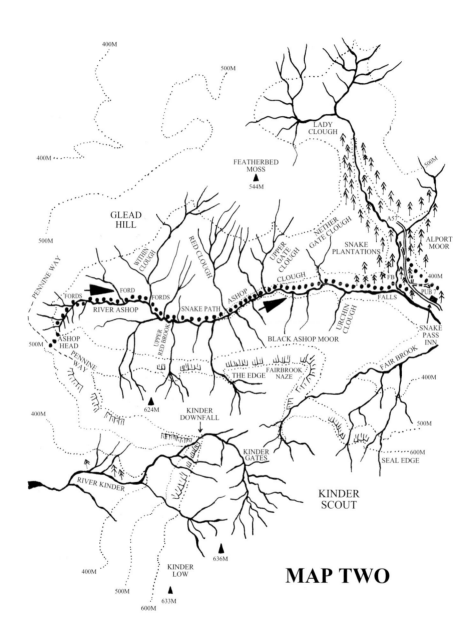

MAP TWO

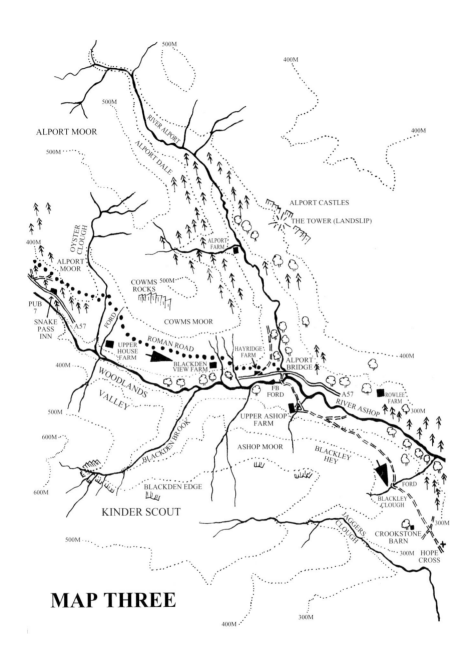

ALPORT MOOR

500M

500M

500M

RIVER ALPORT

ALPORT DALE

ALPORT CASTLES

THE TOWER (LANDSLIP)

ALPORT FARM

OYSTER CLOUGH

ALPORT MOOR

400M

COWMS ROCKS

500M

PUB 7

SNAKE PASS INN

A57

FORD

COWMS MOOR

ROMAN ROAD

UPPER HOUSE FARM

BLACKDEN VIEW FARM

HAYRIDGE FARM

ALPORT BRIDGE

400M

400M

WOODLANDS

VALLEY

FB FORD

A57

RIVER ASHOP

ROWLEE FARM

300M

500M

UPPER ASHOP FARM

600M

BLACKDEN BROOK

ASHOP MOOR

BLACKLEY HEY

600M

BLACKDEN EDGE

BLACKLEY CLOUGH

FORD

KINDER SCOUT

JAGGERS CLOUGH

CROOKSTONE BARN

300M

500M

300M

HOPE CROSS

400M

300M

MAP THREE

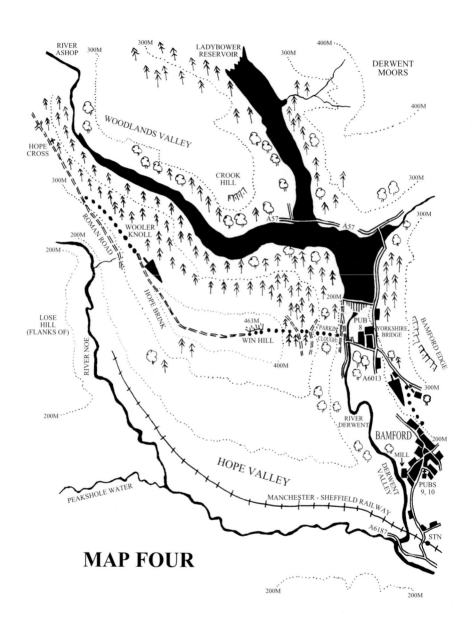

MAP FOUR

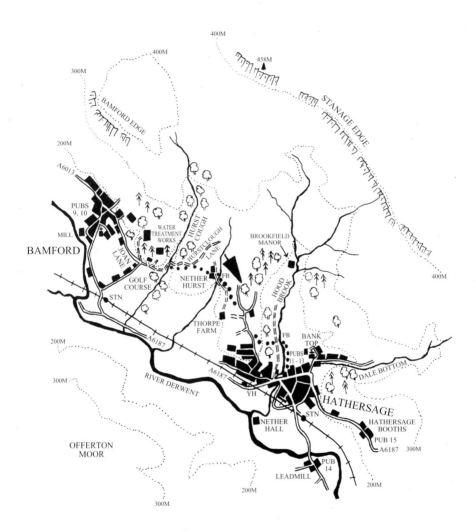

MAP FIVE

HAYFIELD is a delightful mix of Pennine mill town and Peakland village, an outpost of Derbyshire that looks towards Stockport and Manchester. The reason for this contrasting character is its geography for it lies cradled amongst the hills of the Upper Sett Valley in the north-western corner of the Peak District, known locally as the High Peak, with the dramatic escarpment of Kinder Scout tracing across the skyline just to the east forming a physical barrier between Hayfield and the rest of Derbyshire. In Roman times, the road between Buxton and the fort near Glossop came through Hayfield, although the village itself is probably of Saxon origins and was first mentioned as 'Hedfeld' in the Domesday Book when it was little more than a forest clearing. Following the Conquest, this small settlement found itself within the boundary of the Royal Forest of the Peak, a Norman hunting preserve administered from Peveril Castle at Castleton. It remained a small farming community for many centuries, although the forest was gradually encroached upon. Several important packhorse routes across the Pennines also converged here including the busy route between Cheshire and Yorkshire that traversed Kinder Scout by way of Edale Cross (Stage Six of this walk). Things changed dramatically in the 18th Century as demand for woollen cloth grew from the burgeoning towns of Stockport and Manchester. This heralded a period of prosperity as a thriving cottage industry developed with local people weaving cloth in their homes to augment their meagre farming incomes. Houses were rebuilt as three-storey weavers' cottages with handlooms in the light and airy upper floors, several of which still remain. By the early 19th Century, water-powered mills began to take over with several built alongside the River Sett and its tributaries where cotton, rather than wool, was spun. Other industries also sprang up including calico printing, paper mills and quarries. The railway arrived in 1868 linking Hayfield with Manchester, bringing goods to and from the mills and thousands of walkers and tourists at weekends. Up to 5,000 people passed through the station on summer Sundays during the 1920s and 30s. Sadly, the railway closed between New Mills and Hayfield in 1970 but Derbyshire County Council purchased the track-bed and opened the Sett Valley Trail in 1979, with the former station buildings and yard forming a car park and information centre.

Hayfield marked the end of the industrial towns and the start of the hills and will forever be associated with the famous Mass Trespass onto Kinder Scout. On the 24th April 1932 around five hundred ramblers met at Bowden Bridge Quarry just to the east of Hayfield for a rally before their Mass Trespass up onto Kinder Scout in protest at the lack of access to the open hills. For over half a century, there had been growing calls for access to the hills but they remained strictly out of bounds, the preserve of landowners and their gamekeepers. For people living in the industrial towns and cities of Northern England, a days' hill-walking offered fresh air, exercise and freedom away from the mills and factories, but this basic right was denied by an elite who wanted to keep the hills for their grouse. The ordinary folk of Manchester, Sheffield and Stockport gradually became more frustrated at the lack of action and so decided to hold a mass trespass to highlight their plight. They followed the Snake Path up through William Clough then turned off up across the steep slopes towards Sandy Heys only to be met by the Duke of Devonshire's gamekeepers on Kinder Scout. Accounts vary, but a few scuffles broke out and the ramblers continued up onto Kinder Scout where they met a group of Sheffield ramblers who had set off from Edale. After exchanging pleasantries, they returned to Hayfield and Edale only to be met by police at Hayfield who arrested several of the leaders. Five people were subsequently tried at Derby Assizes and sent to prison for up to six months! Such harsh punishment brought widespread condemnation, changed public opinion and united access campaign groups; it even inspired folk singer Ewan McColl to write 'The Manchester Rambler':

"I'm a rambler, I'm a rambler from Manchester way,
I get all my pleasure the hard moorland way.
I may be a wage slave on Monday,
But I am a free man on Sunday."

This was the catalyst for change that led to the National Parks and Access to the Countryside Act 1949, which established this country's National Parks and protected our rights of way. After over 100 years of campaigning, the Countryside and Rights of Way Act was finally passed in 2000 thus allowing access to open hill country, an important piece of legislation that would not have happened if it were not for those

trespassers. *"Kinderscout, at its inconspicuous summit nearly 2100 feet high, is certainly the wildest part of the Peak country, if we waive a doubt as to whether it were actually included in that Péac tribe's bounds. It is also the still least known corner of this region, an effect of various causes. The towns at its base are too busy to lay themselves out for tourists. The roads on its south side do not encourage driving trips. Guide-books, especially those edited by elderly gentlemen, are apt to be much more vague on its features than on those of Buxton and Matlock. Strangers, then, find themselves at a loss what to see and how to get at it. The fact being that the lions of the mountain are not to be seen at all without special permission. It is mostly rented as grouse-moors; on it show few buildings but the miniature castles in which our noble sportsmen encamp themselves against ferocious game; so the doubtful tracks that traverse these preserves become, through part of the year, a war-path between keepers and trespassers, the base sort of whom prove indeed a trial to any proprietor."*
(A. R. Hope Moncrieff, 'The Peak Country', 1908).

In the heart of the village stands St Matthew's Church, a sombre stone building that dates from 1818, its appearance characteristic of the Georgian period. There has been a church on this site since the 14th Century, although previous buildings often succumbed to the floodwaters of the adjacent River Sett. Stories are told of bodies being swept out of their graves by the rising river, which also washed away two bridges. The present bridge was built in 1837 with a much higher arch to prevent flood damage; the power of the river was finally tamed in 1912 when Kinder Reservoir was built upstream. This churchyard was the scene of a 'resurrection' in 1745 when several people reported seeing hundreds of bodies rise from their graves and ascend towards Heaven, an event that was reported in the local newspaper. Close by is Hayfield Cricket Club, which was founded in 1859 but only managed to purchase its ground in 1976 thanks to a fund-raising game between the Hayfield team and some of the cast of Dad's Army including Arthur Lowe, who was born in the village in 1915. Lowe will always be remembered with affection for his portrayal of Captain Mainwaring.

The mills and railway are all but distant memories and Hayfield has returned to a quiet rural village and popular walking base. There are a clutch of great pubs, cafés and interesting shops as well as several old weavers' cottages clustered around the bridge across the River Sett in the heart of the old village. It stands as a classic example of a Pennine mill village that has witnessed the transition from agriculture to home weaving and then small-scale mill spinning. Bring all of these elements together, coupled with its place in walking folklore, and Hayfield is the perfect place to start and finish The Inn Way.

THE SNAKE PATH is an historic route between Hayfield and the Snake Pass Inn via William Clough and Ashop Clough. This footpath holds a special place in the long campaign for access to the hills. During the 19th Century, a growing number of landowners, water companies and railway developers began to exclude people from the hills and banish them from ancient paths and tracks. There were no public bodies to protect such routes and so various footpath societies were established throughout the towns and cities of Northern England to challenge these landowners to uphold the common law usage of these ancient routes. The Peak District and Northern Counties Footpaths Preservation Society was one of the most prominent, formed in 1894 from the much older Manchester Association for the Preservation of Ancient Public Footpaths. Their first task was to secure the long established route from Hayfield to the Snake Pass Inn and the route was formally opened on 29th May 1897 by agreement between the Footpaths Preservation Society and the Duke of Devonshire. The battle to secure access to these hills, something we now take for granted, was long and difficult.

The Snake Path is a delight to walk as it crosses a variety of terrain with ever-changing landscapes of epic proportions. The initial climb out of Hayfield is rewarded with fine views across this old mill village, passing through a number of original wrought-iron gates. A particular feature is the copse of trees known locally as Twenty Trees, although I only counted nineteen! The path then levels out as it crosses Middle Moor, with its conspicuous white-washed Shooting Cabin, before slanting down across White Brow high above Kinder Reservoir. The views across this reservoir are superb with the western escarpment of Kinder Scout dominating and the distinctive peaks of Mount Famine and South Head to the south. Kinder Reservoir was built in 1912 to slake the thirst of Stockport with a capacity of 500 million gallons. During its construction a railway was built to move men and materials from Hayfield Station up alongside the rivers Sett and Kinder to reach the site of the reservoir. A 'tin town' sprung up for the workers near Bowden Bridge, a 16th Century packhorse bridge by the confluence of the rivers Sett and Kinder. From the head of the reservoir, the Snake Path heads up through William Clough, a dramatic moorland ravine where the path hugs the tumbling stream to eventually reach a crossroads of paths at Ashop Head where the Snake Path crosses the route of the Pennine Way. This saddle of land between Mill Hill and the north-west tip of Kinder Scout is the source of the River Ashop, a wild and remote place with moorland all around and the steep escarpment of Kinder Scout dominating. Incidentally, the word 'clough' (pronounced 'cluff') means a narrow ravine whilst the word 'grough' refers to the small stream channels that erode down into the peat hags across the Dark Peak moors.

KINDER SCOUT is where the Pennines really begin, and what a start they get off to! It is a vast plateau of blanket bog and deep gullies that rarely dips below 600 metres, the 'summit' of which stands at 636 metres above sea level, the highest point in the Peak District, although any one of the other hundred or so peat hags could make a claim to the title, indeed several look slightly higher including the nearby OS Trig Point on Kinder Low (633 metres). Shattered gritstone edges run all the way around this plateau falling steeply away into the Woodlands Valley, Vale of Edale, Sett Valley and Ashop Clough. One of the most popular walking areas in Britain, it is a dangerous place with a morass of peat bogs dissected by a maze of deep groughs that will sap your energy and challenge even the most competent navigator. The blanket bog is 7,000 years old, a unique habitat formed when Stone Age people began to clear woodland thus creating wet conditions that allowed peat to form. This fragile landscape is home to sheep, grouse, curlew, golden plover and mountain hare that live amongst the peat hags and groughs. The predominant vegetation is heather, bilberry and cotton grass. It is also prone to erosion through pollution, over grazing and too many boots. Kinder Scout now forms part of the National Trust's High Peak Estate.

THE RIVER ASHOP rises amongst a maze of streams and peat hags on the saddle of land known as Ashop Head between the sweeping moorland of Mill Hill and the north-western tip of Kinder Scout. From Ashop Head, the Snake Path continues its journey from Hayfield to the Snake Pass Inn down alongside the peaty waters of this infant river, initially walking along the boggy riverbed set in a small, shallow valley. The valley gradually becomes deeper, gathering waters from several small streams that tumble down from the escarpment of The Edge that traces the northern rim of Kinder Scout. *"The scenery is impressively grand, but not lovely; although in winter, when the snow wreaths are curled and twisted mysteriously, there is an indescribable, awe-inspiring charm. In certain lights the moors are even weirder that the winding caves of Castleton. There, when dusk of evening falls, one can readily forget the stress of modern life, and believe oneself in the days when metal was unknown and men slew men with weapons of stone. The last cries of grouse and snipe sound hollow and uncanny; the heavy beating of eagle's wings would cause no surprise."* **(R. Murray Gilchrist, 'The Peak District', 1911).** This is walking country par excellence and as wild and untamed as The Inn Way gets, worlds apart from the limestone valleys of the White Peak you will walk through in three days time. The river valley gradually becomes more pronounced as it gathers momentum and soon cuts a dramatic ravine known as Ashop Clough, with sheer slopes and an exciting path. This ravine is short-lived for the character of the valley soon changes as it approaches the Snake Pass (A57) and its confluence with conifer-clad Lady Clough where the waters of the River Ashop are swelled to create a broader river. This change in character is reflected by a change of name for Ashop Clough now becomes the Woodlands Valley. The river now flows south-eastwards through a more pastoral landscape dotted with farms and woodland copse with the northern ramparts of Kinder Scout towering above including the impressive scarps of Fairbrook Naze, Seal Edge and Blackden Edge. Substantial side valleys to the north help drain the vast expanse of Bleaklow, in particular Oyster Clough and Alport Dale.

Before long, the River Ashop begins to back up as it flows into Ladybower Reservoir, a vast expanse of water that floods much of the Woodlands Valley and Upper Derwent Valley. When it was built, it was the largest reservoir in Britain. During its construction between 1935 and 1943 the villages of Derwent in the Upper Derwent Valley and

Ashopton at the confluence of the rivers Ashop and Derwent were both submerged beneath the rising waters - the famous 'lost villages' of the Derwent Valley. The reservoir has a capacity of 6,310 million gallons and supplies drinking water to Sheffield, Leicester, Derby and Nottingham, held back behind a huge dam just upstream of Yorkshire Bridge across the River Derwent. Incidentally, it was Derwent Reservoir further upstream from Ladybower in the Upper Derwent Valley that was used for training by RAF 617 Squadron before their famous Dambuster raids on the Mohne and Eder Dams in Germany during May 1943.

THE SNAKE PASS was built in 1820 under the direction of the great civil engineer Thomas Telford as a toll road between Manchester and Sheffield, now known less romantically as the A57. This was the last of the great Turnpike roads to be built and replaced an old packhorse and coaching route across the Pennines. The Snake Pass refers to the upland section of this route across the lonely High Peak moors between Glossop and the now-submerged village of Ashopton, although its name is not derived from its sinuous curves but from the serpent design on the crest of the Cavendish family, Dukes of Devonshire, who owned much of the surrounding moorland and were instrumental its construction. The historic Snake Pass Inn (originally known as the Snake Inn) was built as a staging post halfway along this tortuous route; tolls were also collected at this inn up until 1870. The inn still serves its original purpose and offers an oasis of warmth and shelter in an otherwise bleak landscape. *"... one of the most remote hostelries in the country, the nearest town to it accessible by road, with the exception of Glossop, being Sheffield which is 17 miles distant. For all that, it is quite capable of giving comfortable entertainment to man and beast."* **(M. J. B. Baddeley, 'The Peak District of Derbyshire and Neighbouring Counties', 1887).**

The Woodlands Valley and Lady Clough have actually been used for thousands of years as a route across the High Peak, indeed the Roman Road between the forts of Navio near Hope and Ardotalia (also known as Melandra Castle) near Glossop came this way. Our walk follows this Roman Road from just above the Snake Pass Inn all the way down through the Woodlands Valley, fording the River Ashop just above its confluence with the River Alport after which it becomes a stony track that climbs steadily up across the eastern flanks of Kinder Scout to reach Hope Cross. The finest stretch of this ancient route is the track from Upper Ashop Farm to Hope Cross from where there are superb views back across the Woodlands Valley, a view that would have been enjoyed by those Roman legions almost 2,000 years ago as they marched across the hills. *"The view from this lofty spot may well have won the admiration even of men whom one imagines so sternly unromantic as the foreign legionaires who must once have come tramping across this pass. Southward it extends, beyond the rich vale of Hope, to the distant moors towards Tideswell and Abney; whilst northward and northwestward the peeps into the Ashop Valley are absolutely without parallel in their character in England, and in loveliness only to be matched in the richest dales in Cumberland or Westmorland."* **(Joseph E. Morris, 'Peak Country', 1914).**

Hope Cross

HOPE CROSS once marked an important crossroads of packhorse routes across the hills between Hope, Glossop, Edale and Sheffield, although originally it stood just to the north of its present site at the crossroads of bridleways. This slender stone guidepost dates from 1737 and replaced a medieval wayside cross, hence its name. Hope Cross stands alongside the Roman Road, which now begins its long and steady descent down into the Hope Valley to the Roman fort of Navio, with superb views across the Vale of Edale and the Great Ridge to the west. This is not a place to linger as the ghosts of Roman soldiers are said to march along this ancient road at dusk and strange lights have been reported in the sky. Just beyond Hope Cross our route leaves the Roman Road and heads steadily up across the broad shoulder of land that sweeps up to the summit of Win Hill. Beyond Wooler Knoll, which is said to take its name from the wolves that once roamed across this high ridge, magnificent views begin to open up across the Hope Valley.

WIN HILL is undoubtedly one of the finest viewpoints in the Dark Peak, its conspicuous summit outcrops crowning a sweeping ridge of moorland that separates the Woodlands, Derwent and Hope valleys. These rocky outcrops, often referred to as the 'pimple', are a famous landmark for miles around and, once climbed, will forever grab your attention as you travel through the area. From its Trig Point a fine view unfolds with the hills of the Great Ridge, Kinder Scout, Derwent Edge and Stanage Edge rising and falling into the distance, whilst far below Ladybower Reservoir floods the Woodlands and Upper Derwent valleys. According to legend, in 626AD the army of King Edwin of Northumbria camped on this rocky summit in preparation for a battle with the forces of King Cwichelm of Wessex and King Penda of Mercia who were encamped on Lose Hill across the valley. The battle ensued and King Edwin was victorious, hence the two names of 'win' and 'lose' hills. A more mundane explanation is that Win Hill is derived from the Saxon word for willow hill. *"Tradition hovers about the place, and tells us that in the dim antiquity of the past, while Edwin ruled Northumbria's land, the armies of two Saxon kings here met in deadly conflict, and the now peaceful valley echoed to the bloody strife and clang of arms. Long and furiously the battle raged, nor ceased the combatants until the waters of the Nowe were crimsoned with the blood of the slain. The victorious army, it is said, encamped where Winhill lifts its stony diadem, the vanquished, on the opposing heights of Losehill."* **(James Croston, 'On Foot through The Peak', 1889).**

From the summit, there is a steep and exciting descent down to reach Yorkshire Bridge across the River Derwent, where 300 metres of height is lost in three-quarters of a mile, with a particularly steep flight of rough steps through the wooded ravine of Parkin Clough; it is quite a relief to reach Yorkshire Bridge. This old stone bridge takes its name from the fact that it was the last river crossing before the Yorkshire border along the old packhorse route between Cheshire and Yorkshire. Centuries ago, this was an important crossing point of the River Derwent. The houses above the bridge were built to re-house people from the drowned villages of Derwent and Ashopton.

BAMFORD is an attractive hillside village situated on south-facing slopes above the River Derwent with the gritstone scarp of Bamford Edge rising above. It is the last remaining of the trio of villages that once graced the Upper Derwent Valley, the other two long since submerged beneath the waters of Ladybower Reservoir. Despite being dissected by a busy road, Bamford retains a village atmosphere with hidden corners, pretty cottages and a pleasant triangular tree-shaded 'green' in the heart of the village. The name of the village literally means 'beam across a ford' and refers to an ancient crossing point of the Derwent that would have been spanned by a simple wooden footbridge. There is still a delightful river crossing by way of stepping stones, wooden planks and a footbridge just below the mill pond beside Bamford Mill, which most probably marks the site of this ancient ford and which may also lie on the line of the Roman road between the forts at Navio and Templeborough. However, some historians believe the 'beam ford' refers to the nearby ancient crossing point of the Derwent that is now occupied by Yorkshire Bridge.

Bamford remained a small agricultural hamlet until the late 18th Century when a cotton mill was built on the site of an earlier corn mill along the banks of the Derwent. Bamford Mill was built in around 1780 although, as with many cotton mills, it burnt down in 1791 due to the highly combustible cotton fibres. The mill was rebuilt in around 1820 by the Moore family, mill owners from Manchester, who invested greatly in the village during the 19th Century providing money for the church, school, village hall and several millworkers' cottages. During its heyday in the 1860s it employed 230 people. Despite fluctuating fortunes, the mill continued to produce cotton products until 1965, after which it operated for a number of years making electric furnaces. It has recently been converted into flats. This historic mill, along with many others along the length of the River Derwent, dates from the earliest years of the Industrial Revolution when mechanised, centralised yarn and cloth production was in its infancy.

St John the Baptist Church, with its pencil-sharp spire, dates from around 1860 and was designed by famous Victorian ecclesiastical architect William Butterfield, who also designed St Paul's Cathedral in Melbourne, Australia. The church is notable for the fact that the deceased from the submerged church at Derwent were re-interred within its churchyard. About three-quarters of a mile to the south of the village lies Bamford Station along the Hope Valley Line. This important railway connects Sheffield with Manchester and was completed in the 1890s by the Midland Railway Company who built it to compete with the older Trans-Pennine route through Longdendale further to the north. This railway has always been instrumental in bringing visitors to the Peak District.

HATHERSAGE is a bustling village set on the slopes of the Derwent Valley with the distinctive outcrops of Higger Tor and Carl Wark rising above and the jagged crest of Stanage Edge dominating the skyline. First settled in Saxon times, the village developed on the rise of land known as Bank Top where the Parish Church now stands, indeed, beside the church are earthworks known as Camp Green that date back to the Dark Ages, although some historians believe these to be early Norman. Its name is derived from the Saxon words for 'ridge settlement', as the higher ground was safer than the thickly wooded and often water logged valleys. A quick glance at the map reveals a wealth of prehistoric remains scattered across the heather moorland above the gritstone edges including enclosures, settlements, stone circles, burial mounds and forts.

The Church of St Michael and All Angels was first mentioned in the early 12th Century, although the present church was built in the 14th Century in Decorated style with some later 15th Century additions by the Eyre family. The Eyre family came over from Normandy with William the Conqueror and subsequently settled in the Hope and Derwent valleys. The family became very influential, especially during the Middle Ages when they held a score of manors throughout the Derwent, Hope and Ashop valleys as well as further a-field. When Sir Robert Eyre returned safely from the Battle of Agincourt in the early 15th Century, it is said he built a manor house for each of his seven sons within sight of the family seat at nearby Highlow Hall and also restored the church as thanksgiving for his safe return. The church is noted for its collection of 15th Century memorial brasses of Sir Robert Eyre and his family. According to legend, a Norman knight called Truelove fought alongside William the Conqueror at the Battle of Hastings. When William was thrown from his horse, his helmet was pushed into his face suffocating him but Truelove came to the rescue and took off his helmet so that William could breathe again, but in doing so lost one of his legs on the battlefield. The future king of England gave Truelove lands in north Derbyshire as a reward for his bravery and then named him 'air' as he had given him air to breathe, hence 'Eyre'. The Eyre coat of arms features a leg in armour.

Hathersage is famed as the last resting place of Little John, "friend and lieutenant of Robin Hood" and one-time resident of Hathersage whose grave can be found in the churchyard. In medieval times, Hathersage stood on the edge of the vast forests of Sherwood and Barnsdale and nearby Loxley is said to have been the birthplace of Robin Hood. Indeed, there are several places locally that bear his name including Hood Brook and Robin Hood's Cave - this whole area was once the stomping ground of England's famed outlaw! In 1784 Little John's grave was opened and a thigh bone measuring 32 inches was allegedly found, large enough for a 7-ft tall man. It is said that his Lincoln green cap and bow hung in the church for many years and that the cottage where he lived and died once stood near the east side of the churchyard. Imagine what a major tourist attraction this cottage would have been if it had not been pulled down during the 19th Century, one of the few buildings to have direct associations with Robin Hood. His grave is tended by the Ancient Order of Foresters. *"The cottage in which he is said to have been born, and to which he wearily returned to die, is evidently of great antiquity. It is a low thatched building, standing within a few yards of the church, and now partially overgrown with ivy and screened by lofty spreading trees. We remember in our earlier visits the house being tenanted by an aged widow, who appeared to place implicit faith in the whole tradition. We have heard her say that she had a distinct recollection of having, in her youth, seen Little John's green cap suspended by a chain in Hathersage Church."* (**James Croston, 1889**).

Hathersage has a long and proud history of Catholicism. The Old Faith remained strong in this corner of Derbyshire during the dark years of the Reformation, practiced by prominent local families such as the Eyres and Fitzherberts. In 1588 John Fitzherbert of Padley Hall was found to be harbouring two Catholic priests within his home. He was arrested and imprisoned for life for this 'crime', although the priests suffered a much worse fate as they were tried at Derby Assize and subsequently hung, drawn and quartered. After this terrible event, the Hathersage home of the Fitzherbert family was used as a secret Mass House. The ascension of James II to the throne in 1685 brought with it greater religious tolerance and so a Catholic chapel was built in Hathersage in 1692, but his reign was short lived and three months after it was built the chapel was destroyed by a Protestant mob. It was not until just over 100 years later that the present Catholic Church of St Michael the Archangel was built in 1806 following various religious emancipation acts during the late 18th Century including the Catholic Relief Act of 1778. Despite these new laws, such was the feeling of unease that this Catholic church was built in a secluded spot set back from the main road behind the George Hotel.

During the Middle Ages Hathersage grew as a stopping point on the busy packhorse routes between Cheshire, Yorkshire and Chesterfield, hence the name of the Scotsman's Pack pub which is a reference to the Scottish linen sold by the travelling traders. Also during this period, lead ore was brought from the primitive mines throughout the White Peak to be smelted on the windy hillsides above Hathersage, which provided both timber and wind to fuel these small smelt mills known locally as boles. Local place-names such as Bole Hill, Lead Hill and Leadmill are evidence of this small-scale industry. Hathersage, however, essentially remained a small agricultural village up until the 18th Century when mills and quarries began to open, attracted by the abundant supply of water power and quality grindstones hewn from the surrounding gritstone edges, particularly Millstone Edge. Hathersage was once a major centre for brass button, needle and wire making and home to England's first needle-making factory in the 1560s. The industry flourished during the 19th Century with five needle mills throughout the village, although working conditions were horrendous with a lethal dust given off by the grindstones as they sharpened the needles. By the turn of the 20th Century, the businesses had moved to Sheffield, although a button factory continued until the 1940s and a number of the old mill buildings still stand throughout the village. *"Hathersage made a bid to become an understudy of Sheffield, being noted a century ago for a local manufacture of needles and steel wire; but luckily for visitors, if not for landowners, its smoke never rose black enough to spoil a fine situation upon heights looking down the Derwent Valley, where the Hood Brook falls in from a wooded glen below Stannage Edge."* **(A. R. Hope Moncrieff, 1908)**

Hathersage has one major literary claim to fame. Charlotte Brontë, one of the famed Brontë sisters of Haworth Parsonage in Yorkshire, stayed with her friend Ellen Nussey at Hathersage vicarage for about three weeks in 1845 and based many of the places and people in her great romantic novel Jane Eyre on her experiences during her stay. She borrowed the surname of the landlord of the George Hotel when she renamed Hathersage as Morton, named the heroine after the prominent local Eyre family and used North Lees Hall as the basis for Thornfield Hall, Mr Rochester's house in her novel. This literary masterpiece was first published in 1847 and became an immediate success, bringing Charlotte fame and wealth. Sadly, she died in 1855 during the early stages of pregnancy aged just 38 years.

Hathersage is a bustling place with good inns, a variety of shops and several attractive buildings along the Main Road, School Lane, The Dale and Church Lane. Look out for the old cheese press near the George Hotel, across the road from which is the ornate Memorial Shuttleworth Lamp Post, erected in 1914 in memory of Colonel Shuttleworth of Hathersage Hall.

STAGE TWO

HATHERSAGE
to
BASLOW

✦

"From Froggatt village, I climbed up through oak woodland and suddenly emerged from the sylvan shade at the base of an impressive wall of gritstone outcrops that seemingly barred my progress. The deeply fissured rock face was festooned with ropes and climbers dangling like giant spiders. I chose the easier way to the crest and followed the gently sloping path up to join a broad track along the top of Froggatt Edge. I triumphantly walked to the scarp-edge to survey my achievement and had one of those 'wow!' moments. I was stood on the crest of a mighty gritstone wave that towered above a dense canopy of trees with the broad Derwent Valley sweeping away. All around were rolling hills, woodland copse, patchwork fields and stone villages; this was England's green and pleasant land."

Mark Reid
October 2005

WALK INFORMATION

Points of interest:	Little John's grave, Jane Eyre and Mr Rochester, an outlaw's hideout, the gritstone crest of a mighty wave, an Iron Age hillfort and Bronze Age circle, a shooting lodge fit for a king, incredible views from Peakland's finest edge, a stone with something to prove and Wellington's monument.

Distance:

Hathersage to Longshaw	6.5 miles
Longshaw to Baslow	6.5 miles
Total	13 miles

Time: Allow 6 hours

Terrain: Field paths and tracks lead up through the valley of Hood Brook to join the road below Stanage Edge. A rough path then climbs up through woodland and across boulders onto Stanage Edge. A wide path follows the top of the Edge (exposed to the elements) all the way to reach its southern end, from where a moorland path leads on to join the road near Upper Burbage Bridge. Moorland paths then skirt above Burbage Brook with a sharp climb onto Higger Tor. The descent from Higger Tor scrambles across boulders. A path then drops down across boggy moorland, over Burbage Brook then up to join a track below Burbage Rocks which is followed to join the A6187. Clear paths and tracks lead across the Longshaw Estate through woodland and across moorland before dropping down to the Grouse Inn. A path then cuts through Hay Wood with a ford across a stream, which may be difficult after rain. The remainder of this walk follows a wide path across the top of Froggatt Edge and Curbar Edge to join Bar Road (stony track) near Wellington's Monument which leads down into Baslow.

Keep away from the edge of Stanage Edge, Froggatt Edge and Curbar Edge - sheer drops and hidden crevices. There are several busy roads to cross - take care on these sections.

Open Access Land:	The path along the top of Stanage Edge heads across Open Access Land. See local signs for information or visit www.openaccess.gov.uk. If this path is unavailable, follow the road skirting below Stanage Edge to reach Upper Burbage Bridge (OS Explorer Map OL1).
	A short section of path through Hay Wood heads across Open Access Land to join up two Rights of Way. This access is by kind permission of the National Trust.
Ascents:	Stanage Edge: 457 metres
	Higger Tor: 434 metres
Viewpoints:	North Lees Hall across the valley of Hood Brook.
	Stanage Edge looking across the Dark Peak hills.
	Higger Tor towards Carl Wark.
	White Edge Moor looking back towards Stanage Edge.
	Froggatt Edge and Curbar Edge.
	Wellington's Monument and the descent along Bar Road.

FACILITIES

Hathersage	Inn / B&B / Shop / PO / Café / Bus / Train / Phone / Toilets / YH / Camp
Stanage Edge	Bus / Toilets
Longshaw	Inn / Shop / Café / Bus / Toilets / Info
Froggatt Edge	Inn / Bus
Baslow	Inn / B&B / Shop / PO / Café / Bus / Phone
	/ Toilets

ROUTE DESCRIPTION

(Map Six)

From the centre of Hathersage, walk up along the main road (A6187) through the village towards 'Dore, Sheffield' then, where the road curves round to the right at the top of the village, turn left along School Lane. Follow this road straight on then, as you reach the Scotsmans Pack, turn left along Church Bank climbing up to reach the entrance gates to the Church. Continue straight on along the lane then, where it bends sharp left around the churchyard, head straight on over a stile beside a gate (on this bend). Follow the wide grassy track straight on then, after 50 yards, take the FP to the left (waymarker post) steeply down the hillside (steps) to reach a slab FB across a stream. Cross the FB and walk straight on alongside the hedge on your left heading up the field then, as the field levels out (waymarker post), bear right up to reach a clear path at the top of the field that leads through undergrowth to quickly reach a stile. Cross the stile and head straight on alongside the field boundary/trees on your left all the way to reach Cowclose Farm. As you reach the farm, head through the gate then follow the path to the right skirting around the buildings to reach a small gate, after which head straight on across the grassy hillside (walking parallel with the farm track just to your left). As you reach the brow of a steep wooded bank above the track (and Hood Brook), follow the path bearing to the right across the wooded hillside to reach a stile that leads onto the road.

Turn left along the road passing North Lees Campsite (and the track towards Cowclose Farm on your left), a short distance after which turn right along a lane (SP) up to reach North Lees Hall. As you reach the Hall, head straight on along the walled track and follow it bending round to the left above the Hall to soon reach a 'junction' of tracks beside a stone waymarker post and information board where you turn right back on yourself slightly along a rough track to quickly reach a gate. Head through the gate and follow the grassy track straight on across the field and through a gate in the far bottom right corner that leads into woodland. Follow the track up through the woods (ravine down to your right) then, as you approach the top of the woods, a path branches up to the left (stone steps) to join the road to the right of a toilet block (Stanage Edge ahead). Head straight across the road along the BW opposite (SP) and follow the grassy path rising up across rough ground to soon join a clear path (stone trod) which you follow up to the right to reach a gate on the edge of Stanage Plantation. A paved trod now bears left up through the woods to reach another gate at the top of the woods, after which a stone-paved path climbs up across the boulder-strewn hillside onto the crest of Stanage Edge. Turn right and follow the path along the top of Stanage Edge (boggy and rocky in places) - the path is level for the first 0.75 miles (keep to the path along the top of the escarpment) then gradually rises up for a further 0.5 miles to reach a Trig Point on top of a large group of outcrops at the southern end of Stanage Edge. As you reach the Trig Point, turn left across the outcrops to quickly pick up a clear path (stone-flagged in places) and follow this down across the boulder-strewn moorland then, as you reach the edge of the outcrops, the path turns down to the right across boulders (easy scrambling). A clear moorland path now leads straight on to join the road near Upper Burbage Bridge.

Head left along the road for a short distance and turn right into the parking area just before Upper Burbage Bridge then almost immediately take the FP to the left through the small gate (SP). After the gate, follow the path to the right heading gently up across the moorland, with Burbage Brook valley falling away to your left. The path levels out after a while and leads on to reach the foot of Higger Tor where a clear path (steps) leads steeply up onto its 'summit' plateau. As you reach the flat 'summit', head left at the junction of paths and follow the wide eroded path, keeping close to the edge on your left, to reach the south-eastern (bottom left) edge of Higger Tor and a small promontory of outcrops. Follow the path down across the outcrops (easy scrambling) to pick up a clear stone-pitched path that leads straight on down across moorland towards the distinctive 'tor' of Carl Wark (Iron Age hill-fort). As you reach the foot of the steep bank of Carl Wark, turn left at the 'crossroads' of grassy paths (at the foot of this bank) and follow this passing below the outcrops/ramparts of Carl Wark on your right. The path soon leaves Carl Wark behind and heads straight down across the boulder-strewn hillside (boggy) to reach a packhorse bridge across Burbage Brook at the bottom of the valley (bottom corner of a plantation on your left). Cross the bridge and follow the clear path straight up across the boulder-strewn hillside to join a clear sandy/grassy track across your path (gritstone edge of Burbage Rocks rising above). Turn right along this track and follow it down through the valley for just over 0.5 miles to reach the main road (A6187).

Cross over the road *(take care)* and head through the small wall-gate opposite (National Trust sign 'Longshaw') and follow the clear grassy path ahead curving round to the left to join a clear wide path which you follow straight on through scattered woodland for 0.25 miles (main road to your left) to reach a white gate that leads onto a road (B6521). Turn right along the road then almost immediately branch off to the left through the entrance gates (National Trust 'Longshaw') and follow the driveway straight on to reach the National Trust Visitor Centre at Longshaw Lodge. *(Detour to the Fox House Inn: Immediately after the entrance gates, turn left back on yourself slightly (by the gatehouse) along a gravel path up through woodland for 200 yards to join the A6187 opposite the Fox House Inn. Retrace your steps back to Longshaw Lodge).* Just before you reach Longshaw Lodge turn left along a gravel track then, where this track forks after a short distance, follow the track ahead curving up to the right passing above Longshaw Lodge. Follow this track gently rising up through woodland to reach a white gate in a wall at the top of the woods. Head through the gate and follow the clear gravel track straight on (to the right) across the Longshaw Estate for just over 0.25 miles then, where the track forks (just after track changes from gravel to grassy), follow the left-hand track gently rising up to reach another white gate in a wall that leads onto the A625 beside its junction with the B6054 at Wooden Pole.

(Map Seven)

Head to the right straight across the road junction *(take care - busy junction)* crossing the small triangular grassy area in the middle of the junction to reach another white gate at the opposite side of the road junction (National Trust sign 'White Edge Moor'). Head through the gate and follow the clear track straight on across the moorland to reach the solitary White Edge Lodge (house). As you approach the house (approx. 50 yards before it), branch off to the left along a grassy path alongside the wall on your left then, where this bends away to the left after a short distance, carry straight on along the clear grassy path across the rough moorland (ignore path off to the left) to join the foot of a low, steep boulder-strewn bank (White Edge) on your left. Follow the clear path along the foot of this bank to reach a gate/stile in a fence just beyond a stream, after which carry straight on gently dropping down for a further 250 yards along the top edge of a small birch wood to reach a junction of paths. Turn right (SP 'Grouse Inn') and follow the path down through the woodland to reach a bridlegate tucked away in the bottom left corner of the field/woods. After the gate, head to the right diagonally down across the middle of the field to reach a bridlegate that leads onto the A625 almost opposite the Grouse Inn.

Turn left along the road passing in front of the Grouse Inn then take the FP to the right over a stile immediately after the pub car park (SP & National Trust sign 'Longshaw Estate'), after which head straight across the field and through a gate in a wall then head diagonally left down across the middle of the field to reach the bottom left field corner where you cross a tumbledown wall to reach a small wall-gate just beyond. After the wall-gate, turn left along the clear path through woodland (Hay Wood) alongside the wall on your left at first then straight on passing Hay Wood car park on your left and down out of the woods to reach a ford across a stream, after which head up along the clear path to quickly reach the A625 *(take care - fast road)*. Turn right along the road for 50 yards then take the track which branches off to the left up through a gate (SP). After the gate, follow this clear track curving round to the left then straight on through birch woodland for 0.5 miles heading across the top of the escarpment to reach a gate in a wall just beyond a stream. Head through the gate and carry straight on along the clear, wide path through scattered birch woodland (stone circle to your left after 300 yards) for approx. 0.25 miles to emerge from the woodland to join the northern end of Froggatt Edge (gritstone escarpment). Carry straight on along the clear path along the top of Froggatt Edge to soon reach some large gritstone outcrops (Froggatt Pinnacle on your right) - continue along the clear, wide path heading along the top of Froggatt Edge. The path soon gently climbs up across outcrops and boulders onto Curbar Edge (keep to the clear, wide path all the way) then continues along the top of Curbar Edge (continuation of Froggatt Edge) for 0.75 miles to eventually reach a kissing-gate beside a white gate at the southern end of Curbar Edge just above the parking area at Curbar Gap (hidden by trees). Head through this gate, just after which the path forks - follow the right-hand track winding down to reach the road at Curbar Gap.

At the road take the stony track opposite up through a bridlegate beside a metal gate (SP), after which head straight on along the broad path alongside the wall on your left, with Baslow Edge just across to your right. After a short distance, follow the broad path gently curving round to the left alongside the wall on your left (ignore the path branching off to the right) gradually bearing away from Baslow Edge then, where this wall turns sharp left, carry straight on along the track across open moorland for a further 0.5 miles to reach the Eagle Stone (large outcrop). Continue straight on along the broad path passing to the right of the Eagle Stone to soon join a clear track (Bar Road) across your path along the top of a wooded escarpment. *(Short detour to the left to reach Wellington's Monument).* Turn right along this track and follow it slanting down across the hillside to reach a gate at the top of an enclosed lane. Head through the gate and follow the lane straight on gently dropping down then, where the lane forks after 0.5 miles, follow the lane bending sharply down to the right (ignore the track to the left towards the barns) and follow this down into Baslow. As you reach the road junction and small triangular green at Over End, either turn left along Eaton Hill down to reach Nether End *(Devonshire Arms and Wheatsheaf Hotel)* or right along School Lane down to reach Bridge End *(Rutland Arms and Rowley's)*.

Hathersage

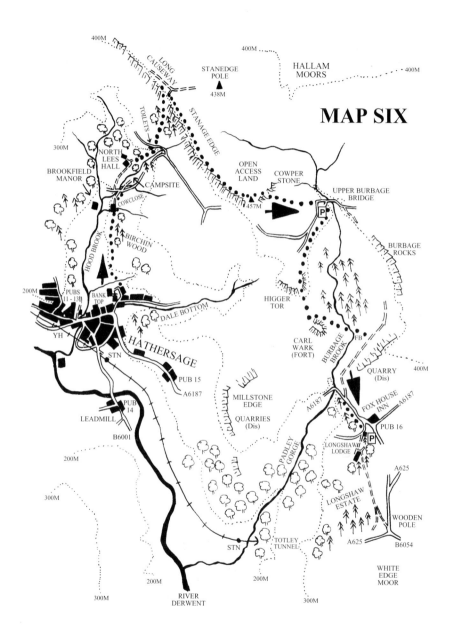

MAP SIX

400M

400M

HALLAM
MOORS

400M

STANEDGE
POLE

438M

LONG CAUSEWAY

TOILETS

STANAGE EDGE

300M

NORTH
LEES
HALL

BROOKFIELD
MANOR

CAMPSITE

COWCLOSE

OPEN
ACCESS
LAND

COWPER
STONE

457M

UPPER BURBAGE
BRIDGE

P

BURBAGE
ROCKS

HOOD BROOK

BIRCHIN
WOOD

200M

PUBS
[11 - 13]

BANK
TOP

DALE BOTTOM

HIGGER
TOR

YH

HATHERSAGE

STN

CARL
WARK
(FORT)

BURBAGE BROOK

FB

QUARRY
(Dis)

400M

PUB 15

A6187

MILLSTONE
EDGE

QUARRIES
(Dis)

A6187

FOX HOUSE
INN

A6187

PUB
14

LEADMILL

PUB 16

P

B6001

LONGSHAW
LODGE

200M

PADLEY GORGE

LONGSHAW
ESTATE

A625

300M

WOODEN
POLE

TOTLEY
TUNNEL

A625

B6054

STN

200M

200M

WHITE
EDGE
MOOR

300M

RIVER
DERWENT

300M

300M

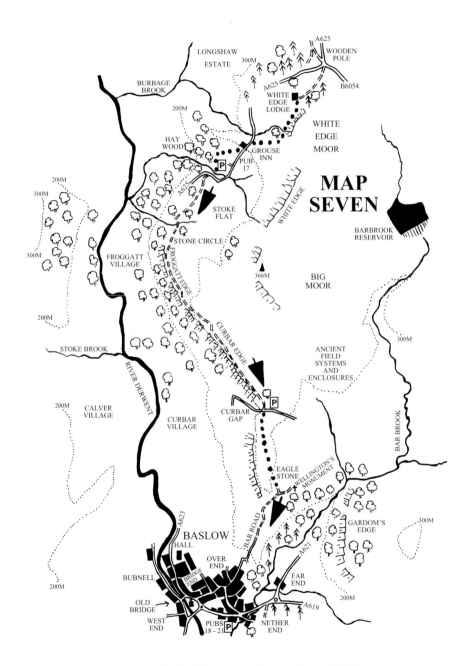

MAP
SEVEN

NORTH LEES HALL is a fine three-storey tower house occupying a commanding position overlooking the valley of Hood Brook with the long crest of Stanage Edge dominating the skyline. The house is thought to have been designed by the famous Elizabethan architect Robert Smythson in 1590 for William Jessop who owned the estate at that time. Smythson was arguably England's first great architect who designed and built several impressive mansion houses, including Hardwick Hall and Wollaton Hall where he used large areas of glazed mullion windows to startling effect, a style that now characterises Elizabethan architecture. Over the centuries, North Lees Hall changed hands several times although its most famous occupants were the Eyre family who lived in the hall from 1750 until 1882. North Lees Hall is most famous for its associations with Charlotte Brontë, who stayed at Hathersage vicarage during 1845. She used North Lees Hall as the basis for Thornfield Hall, Mr Rochester's house in her novel. Her description of Thornfield Hall can be clearly related to North Lees Hall *"It was three storeys high, of proportions not vast, though considerable: a gentleman's manor-house, not a nobleman's seat: battlements round the top gave it a picturesque look. Its grey front stood out well from the background of a rookery, whose cawing tenants were now on the wing: they flew over the lawn and grounds to alight in a great meadow, from which these were separated by a sunk fence, and where an array of mighty old thorn trees, strong, knotty, and broad as oaks, at once explained the etymology of the mansion's designation."* **(Charlotte Brontë 'Jane Eyre' 1847).** The hall was purchased by the Peak District National Park Authority in 1971 and is now used as holiday apartments.

THE OLD PACKHORSE ROUTE between Cheshire and Sheffield climbs up through Stanage Plantation, still paved with gritstone blocks for much of the way, with a final pull up onto the crest of Stanage Edge known as Jacob's Ladder. For many centuries up until 1757 this was the main road between the Hope Valley and Sheffield. The word 'jacob' is derived from 'jagger', the person in charge of a train of packhorses - it is indeed a metaphorical stairway to heaven as the views from Stanage Edge are truly ethereal. This packhorse trod then joins the old Roman road known as the Long Causeway that also traverses Stanage Edge. This road once connected the Roman forts at Brough in the Hope Valley with Templeborough near Rotherham. The Long Causeway crosses the Hallam Moors to the east of Stanage Edge passing Stanage Pole that was used for centuries as a border marker and guidepost; Stanage Edge still marks the boundary between Yorkshire and Derbyshire.

STANAGE EDGE is the longest and the most dramatic of Peakland's eastern edges stretching for over three miles from Stanage End to the Cowper Stone, a huge escarpment of jagged gritstone rocks that rises up from a sea of heather like the crest of a mighty wave. The views are extensive with hills rising and falling as far as the eye can see including Shatton Moor, Mam Tor, Kinder Scout, Win Hill and the brooding moors of the Dark Peak. The Eastern Edges form an almost continuous escarpment tracing high above the Derwent Valley from Howden Edge near the source of the Derwent all the way south to the moors above Baslow and Chatsworth Park, a distance of some twenty miles. 350 million years ago, a warm tropical sea teeming with life covered what is now the Peak District. Over millions of years, countless tiny sea creatures fell to the bottom of this sea and were compressed to form a thick layer of limestone. Then, around 300 million years ago, great rivers flowed over this newly-formed limestone depositing sand and mud which, over time, were compressed to form sedimentary rocks known as gritstones. These rock layers were later pushed up by movements in the earth's plates to form a huge dome, dissected by great river valleys. Over aeons of time, the soft gritstone dome has weathered away so much so that it has completely disappeared in the central and southern areas of the Peak District exposing the limestone beneath, which has created the White Peak landscape. To the north, east and west the dome has remained and now forms the heather moors of the Dark Peak. In the east, the boundary of this weathered gritstone dome has created a vast escarpment of sheer edges - including Stanage, Froggatt and Curbar edges - that tower above the soft, shale river valley of the Derwent.

Rock climbing began here in the 1890s and Stanage Edge is now one of the most famous gritstone edges in the country with hundreds of mapped routes up the countless crevices and outcrops that rise some 30 metres high in places. In summer, the edge is often festooned with ropes and climbers dangling from the rock faces like giant spiders as they tackle some of the more famous climbs including The Unconquerables, Mississippi Buttress, Manchester Buttress, Grotto Slab, Goliath's Groove, The Tippler and the Flying Buttress to name but a few. Keep well away from the edge as there are hidden crevices and sheer drops - and you may also frighten some climbers! Look out for a worn path that leads down to a platform just below the edge with eroded hollows and precarious edges - the farthest hollow is known as Robin Hood's Cave and was possibly one of his many hide-outs. Robin Hood was born at Loxley, a village that lies just six miles to the north-east. Incidentally, Sheffield city centre is only about six miles away as well.

HIGGER TOR dominates the Burbage Valley, a wonderful flat-topped natural tor of more resistant gritstone rock fringed by outcrops, crags and boulders, although some historians suggest that this was an ancient ritualistic site perhaps associated with nearby Carl Wark. *"The sombre mass of blackened crags standing out upon the lonely moor looks primevally wild and forbidding, and you can hardly wonder at the superstitious belief that here the Druid priests of old performed their sacrificial rights before the wild and fiery Britons."* **(James Croston, 'On Foot through The Peak', 1889).** This prominent landmark is visible for miles around, its distinctive profile one of the more easily identifiable natural rock features along the whole of the Eastern Edges. The views from its summit plateau are extensive with a particularly fine panorama across the Burbage Valley towards Carl Wark just to the south. The name of Higger Tor is simply a derivation of 'higher tor'.

CARL WARK is a completely natural but perfectly-formed flat-topped tor, slightly smaller in stature than neighbouring Higger Tor but visually just as impressive as it rises boldly from its moorland surroundings with jagged rocks and boulder-strewn slopes. It was used from the Iron Age (800 BC) through to the Dark Ages as a hill-fort, although historians are still uncertain as to its precise age and history. This small plateau is surrounded on three sides by rocky boulder-strewn slopes that fall steeply away towards Burbage Brook providing natural defences whilst a stone wall and earth bank rampart were built to defend its western side, which can still be seen. Carl Wark is one of the finest prehistoric defensive sites in the Peak District and a fascinating place to explore. *"...a rude fort built upon the brow of the hill by the skin-clad warriors of old Britain..."* (**James Croston, 1889**). Sit awhile on its eastern edge overlooking the Burbage Valley and let your imagination journey back over two millennia to a long forgotten way of life. This mysterious hill-fort is thought to have given this area its name for Burbage may be derived from 'burh' the Saxon work for a defensive site.

BURBAGE BROOK is a small moorland stream that flows through the delightful Burbage Valley on its way to swell the waters of the Derwent with a dramatic finale through the deep ravine of Padley Gorge, its steep sides cloaked with ancient oak woodland. Just to the east of Carl Wark is a delightful old stone packhorse bridge that spans Burbage Brook, which once formed part of a busy packhorse route between Sheffield, Dore and Hathersage. This is a particularly fine example of a packhorse bridge as it does not have any sides, which allowed laden packhorses to cross unhindered. The Burbage Valley is hemmed in to the east by a line of gritstone crags known as Burbage Rocks, beneath which runs a track-way known as the Duke's Drive that was built to enable the Duke of Rutland's shooting parties to reach the surrounding moors from his shooting lodge at Longshaw. Burbage Rocks was once a centre of millstone production, along with many other of the eastern Edges in particular Millstone Edge above Hathersage. This industry can be traced back to medieval times, although simple quernstones (grinding stones worked by hand) for bread-making had been produced from local gritstone since prehistoric times. The industry reached its peak between the 16th and 18th Centuries, particularly when the Turnpike routes to Sheffield and Chesterfield opened and thus increased demand for quality millstones and grindstones that were used for a variety of purposes including grinding cereals, pulping apples for cider as well as in the manufacture of glass and paint and within the flourishing iron and steel industries. Derbyshire millstones were even exported abroad and were used in Scandinavia to pulp timber. However, the industry came to an end during the late 19th Century as alternatives to millstones were found and also because it became fashionable to eat white bread rather than the grey bread Peak District millstones produced! Suitable rocks were quarried from the rock face and then fashioned in situ before being transported across the moors to Sheffield and beyond. Some partly completed millstones were abandoned in the quarries due to imperfections and can still be seen. Such was the importance of this industry that a millstone was adopted by the Peak District National Park Authority as its logo.

THE LONGSHAW ESTATE is a large swathe of countryside owned and managed by the National Trust that includes open moorland, ancient woodland and working farms situated high above the confluence of Burbage Brook and the River Derwent. The history of Longshaw Estate dates back to the early years of the 19th Century when the Duke of Rutland developed it as his own private shooting estate that covered over 11,500 acres from Burbage Moor in the north to Birchen Edge in the south, with shooting rights over an additional 2,200 acres. Longshaw Lodge was built in 1827 as a lavish shooting lodge where the Duke could entertain his many distinguished guests that included King George V and the Duke of Wellington. The Lodge had its own chapel, large stable block and servants' quarters and the Duke also had a network of private carriage-ways built across the estate. The Duke of Rutland travelled to Longshaw Lodge from Haddon Hall near Bakewell, his Derbyshire country manor house that has been in the family since the 12th Century. The Vernon family came over to England with William the Conqueror and they held the Haddon estate until the 16th Century when it passed to the Manners family following the marriage of Dorothy Vernon to Sir John Manners, son of the Earl of Rutland. They subsequently became the Dukes of Rutland and spent much of their time at Belvoir Castle in Leicestershire especially during the 18th and 19th Centuries, although Haddon Hall remained their Derbyshire home. In 1927, the Duke put the Longshaw Estate up for sale with plans to build houses on part of it and even a golf course! Over 3,000 acres of moorland as well as the grounds surrounding the Lodge were bought by Sheffield Corporation for water collection purposes, however, after a fund-raising campaign to save the Estate almost 750 acres of land, which now forms the heart of the Longshaw Estate, were bought and handed to the National Trust in 1931. Longshaw Lodge is now private flats but there is an Information

Centre and café as well as many wonderful walks through the Estate. Longshaw Meadow, in front of the Lodge, is the home of the annual Longshaw Sheepdog Trials held every September. These are the oldest sheepdog trials in the country that date back to 1898. *"As a moorland vignette I know of no place more perfect than the valley of the Burbage, a brown lively stream that gathers together on the uplands between Sheffield and Hathersage. At some slight distance is Longshaw Lodge, the shooting box of the Duke of Rutland, which boasts perhaps the best situation of any house in the district. With its heavy background of trees this quaint irregular place scarce seems real - one might be looking upon some strange old woodcut."* **(R. Murray Gilchrist, 'The Peak District', 1911).**

Our route through Longshaw Estate follows a number of fine tracks, originally built as private carriageways for the Duke's shooting parties, with several white gates known as the Duke's Gates that were designed to be opened by a mounted horse-rider. Up until the 1830s, the Turnpike road between Dronfield and Tideswell came right through the estate but the Duke had it moved to its present course via the Fox House Inn when he bought the Estate and then changed the old Turnpike road into one of his private carriageways. Our route through Longshaw Estate follows this former Turnpike road - look out for the 18th Century guidepost near the entrance gatehouse just off the B6521 which once marked the crossroads of routes between Sheffield, Dronfield, Hope and Tideswell; note the phonetic spelling. This old Turnpike road joins the present-day road junction (A625 and B6054) beside Wooden Pole, which was originally erected to guide travellers across the moors; the present pole is a modern replica although there is evidence that a waymarker pole has been sited here since medieval times.

WHITE EDGE MOOR was bought by the National Trust in 1974 from the North Derbyshire Water Board and added to their Longshaw Estate. This boulder-strewn moorland boasts a variety of wildlife including upland birds such as snipe and red grouse as well as adders, Britain's only poisonous snake, and some deer that have escaped from Chatsworth Park. The views are extensive with far-reaching vistas across the Eastern Edges towards Higger Tor and Burbage Brook. The solitary White Edge Lodge was originally built as the gamekeeper's cottage as part of the Duke of Rutland's Longshaw Estate but is now used as a National Trust holiday cottage.

STOKE FLAT is a gently shelving swathe of moorland sandwiched between Froggatt Edge and White Edge which, along with the many other more extensive areas of moorland that stretch to the east of the Edges including Big Moor and East Moor, is littered with a wealth of prehistoric remains. There are clearance cairns, ancient field systems, standing stones, stone circles and burial mounds that date back to the Bronze Age. They often chose elevated, open spaces for their spiritual and ceremonial monuments and Stoke Flat is no exception with the remains of a large stone circle just off the main path at the northern end of Froggatt Edge. The circle comprises around a dozen stones, many of which have fallen and are quite small with the exception of one large standing stone that probably marked the entrance to the circle, which is then ringed by an earthen bank. The feature of this stone circle is the vast open sky all around, as it is thought that it was built to interpret the passage of the sun and moon across the sky during the solstices.

FROGGATT EDGE, along with its southern and slightly higher neighbour of Curbar Edge, forms a continuous wall of gritstone crags than run for over one and a half miles from Stoke Flat to Curbar Gap. These are perhaps the most popular of the eastern gritstone edges as the path along the top offers a wonderful high-level route with incredible views across the Derwent Valley. From north to south, there is a magnificent panorama across the eastern Peak District with Win Hill, Stanage Edge, Higger Tor, Middleton Dale, Coombs Dale, Calver and Chatsworth Park clearly visible. The most impressive section is around Froggatt Pinnacle, a detached turret of gritstone that proudly juts out from the Edge near where the footpath from the Chequers Inn climbs up out of the Derwent Valley through oak woodland that cloaks the hillside just below the Edge. This is undoubtedly one of the finest walks in England, an exhilarating and breezy promenade along the crest of the Edge from where the views are so breath-taking that you feel compelled to stop and drink it in from every vantage point. Froggatt Edge is second only to Stanage Edge in popularity amongst rock climbers, and is noted for its large rock slabs with over 150 named routes such as Sunset Slab and Three Pebble Slab. Again, take care as there are hidden crevices and sheer drops. At its southern end, the old Turnpike road between Tideswell and Chesterfield takes advantage of a natural 'saddle' along the edges known as Curbar Gap.

THE EAGLE STONE is situated near the southern end of Baslow Edge, a large tor of resistant gritstone that stands sentinel above the heather moorland. The first thing that strikes you is that it looks nothing like an eagle, which is probably due to the fact that it takes its name from the Celtic god Aigle! This large stone is said to turn round each morning at cock-crow, a reminder of when our prehistoric ancestors used it to worship the rising sun; over the centuries, ancient pagan customs and ceremonies such as this have been diluted and trivialised into a more easily understood version. Another local tradition was for the young men of Baslow to climb to the top of the stone to prove their prowess before they were deemed fit to marry!

Wellington's Monument

WELLINGTON'S MONUMENT lies just to the south of the Eagle Stone, a large stone cross situated on a gritstone outcrop overlooking the side-valley of Bar Brook. It was built to commemorate the Duke of Wellington in 1866 by Mr Wrench, a Baslow doctor who had previously served as an army surgeon in Crimea and India. Across the valley on Birchen Edge is another monument dedicated to the memory of Lord Nelson. The track that leads down from Wellington's

Monument into Baslow is known as Bar Road and was once the main packhorse route between Baslow, Sheffield and Chesterfield. Beside this old track-way is Lady Wall Well where horses would refresh before the long climb up onto the moors.

BASLOW is a bustling village that stands watch over the northern entrance to Chatsworth where several important routes converge to cross the River Derwent, which explains the large number of old coaching inns to be found throughout the village. To the north are the gritstone edges of the eastern moors running in a continuous escarpment for many miles towards the source of the Derwent, whilst to the south are the undulating pastures of Chatsworth Park. *"The number of well-to-do, fair-sized inns which the village possesses is due to its position at a main entrance to Chatsworth from Sheffield and other places in that direction. During the season two or more coaches or omnibuses leave for Sheffield every evening; one at 7 o'clock by the direct route through Owler Bar, and one at 6 by the round-about, but more picturesque, Froggatt Edge route. Fares by either route, 1s. 6d."* **(M. J. B. Baddeley, 'The Peak District of Derbyshire and Neighbouring Counties', 1887).**

Baslow is made up of several 'separate' settlements including West End, Bridge End, Over End, Nether End and Far End, each with their own distinctive character. The oldest part is Bridge End where there has been a ford across the Derwent since the earliest times, later replaced by a wooden bridge that was replaced in 1603 by the present three-arched Old Bridge. Beside this bridge is the tiny Watchman's Hut where the village men would guard this important river crossing and where tolls were also collected. Interestingly, this is the only bridge along the Derwent not to have been washed away by floods. This Old Bridge has now been bypassed by the more modern Devonshire Bridge just downstream. Close by is St Anne's Church set in a lovely spot beside the Derwent, with its squat spire, battlemented parapets and unusual clock face with 'VICTORIA 1897' rather than numerals that was a gift of Baslow doctor Mr Wrench to commemorate Queen Victoria's Diamond Jubilee. This site has been used as a place of worship since pre-Conquest days, however, the present church dates from around 1300 when the spire and nave were built, although alterations were made in the 19th Century by the Duke of Devonshire. The church is noted for its preserved dog whip that was once used to drive stray dogs from the church during services, or perhaps to wake up some of the snoring congregation!

Nether End clusters around the northern entrance to Chatsworth Park, a village in itself with shops and inns overlooking Goose Green. The path into Chatsworth Park crosses an old bridge across Bar Brook just beyond which is a row of thatched cottages, a rarity in Derbyshire. This part of Baslow is closely linked to the Chatsworth Estate, although up until the 19th Century much of Baslow, in particular Nether End, formed part of the Duke of Rutland's estate. Over the years they have sold off land and buildings to the Chatsworth Estate as well as local people, although the Duke of Rutland's influence remains in Bridge End with the Rutland Arms. Just up from Goose Green is the Cavendish Hotel, which dates back to the 1780s when it was a renowned coaching inn owned by the Duke of Rutland known as the Peacock Inn that served travellers along the Chesterfield to Buxton Turnpike road. The inn was purchased by the Duke of Devonshire in the 1830s. During the 1970s the inn was rebuilt as the Cavendish Hotel by the Chatsworth Estate with décor and furnishings personally selected by the Duchess. It is now one of Derbyshire's finest hotels. The once famous Hydropathic Hotel was situated in the Over End area of Baslow at the foot of Bar Road. As communications improved and wealth increased during the late 19th Century, more and more people sought cures away from the grimy cities and towns, which often combined fresh air, countryside and hydrotherapy. The Hydropathic Hotel opened in 1881 and flourished in the decades up until the First World War, however, the fashion for hydrotherapy waned during the 1920s and the hotel fell into disrepair and was demolished in the 1930s; only the stone gateposts remain. Nearby is Baslow Hall, home of Sebastian de Ferranti between 1913 and his death in 1930. De Ferranti was an electrical engineer and inventor who most famously pioneered centralised large-scale electrical generation and distribution. He designed and built Deptford Power Station, the first high-voltage generation station in the world that brought electricity to central London using AC transmission, a system that is still in use today throughout the world. The hall is now a prestigious hotel and restaurant.

BASLOW
to
YOULGRAVE

✦

"It was one of those magical winter's days when the slanting sun picked out every contour with deep shadows that gave depth to the landscape. The rocks and crags became even more dramatic, picked out on the crest of a hill by the faltering rays of sunlight. Through skeletal birch trees laid bare by winter's grip, I made my way across Stanton Moor until I reached a small clearing where before me was a ring of nine standing stones. Four millennia ago, our ancestors built this stone circle to honour the solstices and the passing of the sun; they had noticed the power of the sun, its light and shadow just as I had done walking across the moor. Their forgotten way of life seemed distant yet somehow all around, still there with the sun's passage across the winter sky."

Mark Reid
January 2006

WALK INFORMATION

Points of interest:	Chatsworth Park and Capability Brown, the Palace of the Peak, a hotchpotch of buildings, a mournful visit by JFK, the tale of two dukes, a marooned station, hillside villages and classic Peakland pubs, mystical moorlands, a Druid's temple, a hermit's cave and a leaping outlaw.

Distance:

Baslow to Rowsley	5.5 miles
Rowsley to Youlgrave	6.5 miles
Total	12 miles

Time: Allow 6 hours

Terrain: Between Baslow and Beeley, this walk heads across Chatsworth Park following clear tracks and paths through scattered woodland and along the banks of the River Derwent. From Beeley, field paths lead steeply up into Smeltingmill Wood. A wide path and then a track lead through these woods (steep drops to side of path in places) to join Chesterfield Lane from where a path leads down to join the A6 at Rowsley. From Rowsley, field paths and country lanes lead up through Congreave and Stanton in Peak onto Stanton Moor, with a couple of short but steep sections. Clear paths then lead through woodland and across moorland to reach Birchover from where undulating field paths (muddy in places) lead across Harthill Moor all the way to Youlgrave. *Take care exploring Rowtor Rocks, Cratcliff Tor and Robin Hood's Stride – sheer drops and hidden crevices. Take care when walking along roads around Stanton in Peak as well as crossing busy roads at Beeley, Rowsley and Birchover.*

Ascents:	Smeltingmill Wood:	215 metres
	Stanton Moor:	307 metres
	Harthill Moor:	250 metres

Viewpoints	Chatsworth Bridge looking towards Chatsworth House.
	Fields above Congreave looking across the confluence of the rivers Wye and Lathkill.
	Stanton Moor looking across the Derwent Valley.
	Extensive views from Robin Hood's Stride.
	Descent towards Youlgrave from Harthill Moor.

FACILITIES

Baslow	Inn / B&B / Shop / PO / Café / Bus / Phone / Toilets
Chatsworth House	Shop / Café / Bus / Toilets
Edensor	Shop / Café / Bus
Beeley	Inn / B&B / Shop / Café / Bus / Phone
Rowsley	Inn / B&B / Shop / PO / Café / Bus / Phone / Toilets / Camp
Stanton in Peak	Inn / Bus
Birchover	Inn / B&B / Shop / Bus / Phone / Toilets / Camp
Youlgrave	Inn / B&B / Shop / PO / Bus / Phone / Toilets / YH / Camp

ROUTE DESCRIPTION

(Map Eight)

From Goose Green in the Nether End area of Baslow (with your back to the car park and Goose Green in front of you) turn right along the road then, where it bends round to the left at the end of the green (café on corner), take the turning straight on ('Dead End' sign) over a bridge across Bar Brook. After the bridge, turn immediately right along a lane (SP 'Chatsworth') passing in front of some thatched cottages and through a metal squeeze-stile beside a gate, after which follow the wide gravel path straight on then skirting to the left around Plantation Cottage to reach the Cannon kissing-gate (revolving metal gate) on the edge of Chatsworth Park. Head through the gate and follow the wide path straight on (SP 'Chatsworth House, Queen Mary's Bower') to soon join a metalled lane, which you follow straight on to reach a crossroads of lanes/tracks beside White Lodge gatehouse. Continue straight on along the gravel track heading across Chatsworth Park for a further 0.75 miles to reach the road beside Chatsworth Bridge just beyond Queen Mary's Bower (Chatsworth House across to your left).

Turn right over Chatsworth Bridge across the River Derwent, immediately after which follow the gravel path branching off to the right gradually bearing away from the road. Follow this path gently rising up across Chatsworth Park, through an area of scattered trees then down passing above the solitary Park Cottage to reach the B6012 opposite Edensor village. Turn left along the B6012 heading across Chatsworth Park (unenclosed road) then, where the main road bends sharply round to the right, turn left along the entrance driveway towards Chatsworth House. Follow this driveway for 25 yards passing the small triangular road junction on your right then, where this driveway bends down to the left just after the triangular junction, head straight on across Chatsworth Park (no clear path). Head straight on across the parkland bearing very slightly to the left down across the gently sloping hillside to join a clear path along the banks of the River Derwent on your left. Follow this riverside path downstream, passing a derelict mill after which continue down alongside the river to join the road beside One Arch Bridge across the River Derwent. Turn left over the bridge then immediately right through a kissing-gate (SP) and follow the path, flanked with trees, straight on to re-join the road opposite Beeley Church.

Cross the road *(take care - fast road)* and follow the lane opposite passing St Anne's Church on your left up into Beeley then, at the junction just after the Church, turn right then right again down to reach the Devonshire Arms. Pass in front of the pub then turn left immediately after it (SP 'Beeley Moor') and follow the road up out of the village leaving the houses behind then take the FP to the right through a small gate in the hedge (SP). Head straight on alongside the fence on your right and through a gate, after which turn left up alongside the fence on your left to reach a squeeze-stile at the top of the field. After the stile, bear right up through another squeeze-stile in a wall, after which slant up across the hillside to join a track that leads to a gate on the edge of Burnt Wood. Head into the woods then, after a few paces, follow the right-hand level path heading through the woods then, where the path forks again after 150 yards, follow the left-hand narrow path heading straight on through the trees to soon join a wide path which you follow up to the left through a gap in a large retaining wall set in a disused quarry. Follow the path straight on *(ignore path to left after the retaining wall)* to soon reach a FB to your right over Smeltingmill Brook, after which follow the path gently dropping down with the wooded ravine to your right at first then bearing left through the woods up to join a track across your path (SP) - *ignore FP to right just before this track.* Turn right along this track and follow it through the woods then, where it bends down to the right to a gate at the end of the woods that leads onto a road (Chesterfield Lane), branch off to the left through the woods to quickly reach a bridlegate in a fence (Toll Bar Cottage just ahead)*. Head through the bridlegate and walk straight across the garden skirting behind the house and through a gate that leads onto the road (Chesterfield Lane). Turn right down along the road passing in front of Toll Bar Cottage just beyond which (after the entrance to Woodside), take the FP to the left through a squeeze-stile (SP 'Little Rowsley'). Follow this path straight on down across the hillside, enclosed for most of the way, to join the main A6 road at Rowsley.

* At the time of writing there is an application to divert the bridleway so that it follows the track all the way down to join Chesterfield Lane rather than cutting across the gardens behind Toll Bar Cottage. If this diversion is granted then the bridleway will be clearly marked down along the track to Chesterfield Lane, where you will then turn left for a few paces then right along the FP (SP 'Little Rowsley') just before the entrance to Woodside.

Turn right along the A6 towards 'Buxton, Manchester', over the bridge across the Derwent after which turn left along School Lane towards 'Stanton in the Peak' *(use pelican crossing to cross the road)*. Follow this road passing the school then Caudwell's Mill and straight on over a bridge across the River Wye after which follow the road bending round to the right. Follow this road straight on with the River Wye on your right then, where this road bends sharply up to the left, head straight on (off this bend) through a small wall-gate beside a field gate. After the gate, head straight on alongside the River Wye for 25 yards then follow the grassy path bearing slightly to the left up across the hillside (waymarker) through an area of scattered trees (leaving the river behind). Follow this clear path straight on gently rising up across the hillside (River Wye across to your right) to join a grass-covered bank and ditch on your left (just after a solitary stone gatepost). Continue along the clear path alongside this bank and ditch gently curving round to the left for 100 yards then bear off to the right (waymarker) across the field to reach a small wall-gate tucked away in the field corner at the bottom end of a small wood. After the wall-gate, follow the path down to the right and through a small gate either side of a stream, after which head straight on bearing to the right across the hillside and follow this hillside curving round to reach a gate near some barns that leads onto a grassy track which you follow to quickly reach the road through Congreave. Turn left along the road and follow this winding steeply up bending sharply to the right then the left and round to the right again then, where the gradient eases, take the FP to the right (SP) over a stile in a hedge beside a field gate. After the stile, head up across the field alongside the wall on your left to reach a small gate in the top corner of this field, after which carry straight alongside a line of large trees on your left then, where these trees end, continue straight on heading steeply up across the field and up some steps that lead onto Pilhough Lane. Turn right along this road and follow it for 0.5 miles into Stanton-in-Peak.

As you reach the road junction in the centre of the village with the entrance gates to Stanton Hall opposite *(pub short detour to the right)* turn left towards 'Stanton Lees, Birchover'. Head up along the road through the village with the estate wall on your right then, as you near the top of the village where the road bends to the right, take the narrow lane branching off to the left towards 'Stanton Lees'. Follow this road climbing up out of the village then heading steadily up through woodland - the road emerges from the woodland and levels out where you take the FP to the right (just after the quarry track) through a small gate beside a field gate (SP 'Footpath via Stone Circle'). After the gate, head straight on along the grassy track across two fields to reach a gate on the edge of woodland (Stanton Moor Plantation), after which continue straight on along the track along the edge of the woodland to reach another gate. Head through the gate and carry straight on along the clear path heading through silver birch woodland then curving gently round to the right to reach Nine Ladies Stone Circle set in a clearing on your right (information board). At the stone circle, carry straight on along the clear path (stone circle to your right) to soon emerge from the birch woodland where you continue straight on along the wide path heading across Stanton Moor for 0.5 miles to reach a 'crossroads' of paths (moorland begins to drop down) where you follow the wide path to the right to reach the solitary gritstone outcrop of the Cork Stone (hand-grips). At the Cork Stone, carry straight on along the clear path alongside a fence on your left down over a stile and through a short section of woodland to join Birchover Road. Turn left along the road and follow this down to reach the buildings and entrance to Birchover Quarry just after which turn right through the parking area (SP) and straight on along the footpath ahead. Follow this clear path straight on heading steadily down through woodland for 0.25 miles then, where the path forks beside a wall corner on your left (SP), turn left down steps and along an enclosed path passing to the left side of the Red Lion Inn to emerge onto the Main Street in the centre of Birchover.

Turn right down along the Main Street then, where the road bends to the right at the bottom of the village (by the Druid Inn), take the turning to the left heading straight on ('Dead End' sign) passing the Druid Inn on your right then down passing Birchover Church on your left and follow the narrow lane down to reach a junction of lanes beside the entrance to the Old Vicarage. Carry straight on along the track ahead towards Rocking Stone Farm then, where this track bends sharply round to the left, head straight on along the rutted grassy track ahead then where this forks after approx. 50 yards bear left up to quickly reach a wall-stile beside a gate. Head through the gate and follow the enclosed grassy track straight on passing an old barn just after which the track curves round to the left to reach a gate across the track and a bridlegate just off the track to the right (SP). Head through this bridlegate (do not continue along the track) and follow the path straight on slanting down across the hillside through undergrowth to reach a stile in the bottom field corner that leads onto the B5056 road *(take care)*. Turn left along the road for approx. 200 yards then, as the road sweeps round to the left, take the turning to the right to quickly reach a crossroads of tracks/lanes after a few paces where you turn right through a gate that leads onto a driveway. Follow this driveway steadily up to reach a gateway at the top of the field, after which head straight on up across the field alongside the field boundary on your left (do not follow the driveway towards Cratcliff Cottage) to reach a gate in the top corner of the field. Head through the gate and follow the enclosed rough track up to soon reach the end of the enclosed track at the top of the hill, with the outcrops of Robin Hood's Stride up to your left.

Short detour to the Hermit's Cave - cross the wall-stile to the right just before the top of the track, after which follow the path keeping close to the fence/woodland on your right climbing up at first then straight on to reach a wall-stile that leads out onto an area of outcrops and woodland (Cratcliff Tor). After the wall-stile pick your way between the boulders and trees to the right dropping down then skirting just below the boulders through trees to quickly reach the Hermit's Cave. Re-trace your steps back to the top of the rough track near Robin Hood's Stride.

At the top of the enclosed rough track, cross the stile to the left (with Robin Hood's Stride up to your left) and walk straight on for 10 yards then cross the wall-stile to the right beside a gate. After the wall-stile, head diagonally to the left across the middle of the field to reach a wall-stile near a gate in the bottom left field corner, after which head to the left across the field *(Nine Stones stone circle across to your right in the next field)* to reach a gate that leads onto the road opposite the entrance to Harthill Moor Farm. At the road, head straight on along the farm lane (SP 'Youlgreave') to reach a junction of tracks just before the buildings of

Harthill Moor Farm. Turn left at this crossroads along the track for approx. 25 yards then turn right just before the large barns and over a stile beside a gate, after which head straight on keeping close to the wall on your right to quickly reach a stile immediately to the right of a double metal gate (do not follow the rough track down the hillside). After the stile, carry straight on across the upper flanks of the steep hillside *(Castle Ring hill-fort up to your right)* then, after 75 yards (waymarker post), follow the narrow path bearing slightly to the left slanting down across the steep hillside (waymarkers) to reach a small gate beside a field gate at the bottom of the grassy valley (SP). After the gate, head to the right along the grassy path gently rising up across the hillside then curving round to the left (following the hillside) and down to reach a solitary squeeze-stile/gatepost at the foot of the steep bank. At this solitary gatepost, head to the right straight down across the middle of the field (heading towards the centre of Youlgrave in the distance), over a solitary stile set in an old hedge-line then carry straight on down to reach a stile/wooded stream (Bleakley Dike) at the bottom of the field. After the stream, head straight on bearing very slightly to the right across the field (heading towards the tower of Youlgrave Church) to reach a gate in the far right field corner, after which head straight on alongside the wall on your right to reach a squeeze-stile beside a gate in the bottom corner of the next field. After this gate, follow the track to the right and through another gateway, after which head straight across the field to join the wall on your right which you follow straight on then, three-quarters of the way across this field, head through the squeeze-stile to the right after which bear left across the field and through another squeeze-stile that leads onto the road opposite some houses on the very edge of Youlgrave. Turn right down along the road and over a bridge across the River Bradford immediately after which turn left alongside the river to quickly reach a gate (SP) that leads onto a riverside path. Follow this riverside path straight on then, after 150 yards, follow the clear path slanting up to the right across the steep hillside to reach a squeeze-stile at the top of the steep bank where you follow the enclosed path straight on to quickly join a lane which you follow straight on to emerge onto the Main Street opposite the Old Hall. Turn right into the centre of Youlgrave.

Baslow

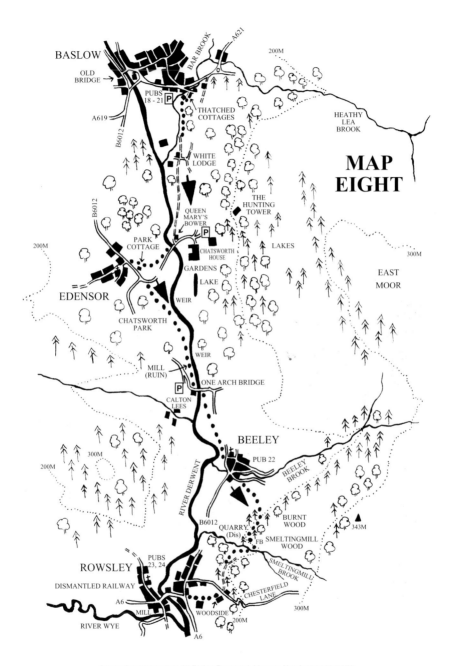

MAP EIGHT

BASLOW

OLD BRIDGE

PUBS 18 - 21

A619

B6012

THATCHED COTTAGES

WHITE LODGE

QUEEN MARY'S BOWER

PARK COTTAGE

CHATSWORTH HOUSE

GARDENS

LAKE

WEIR

EDENSOR

CHATSWORTH PARK

WEIR

MILL (RUIN)

ONE ARCH BRIDGE

CALTON LEES

BAR BROOK

A621

200M

HEATHY LEA BROOK

THE HUNTING TOWER

LAKES

300M

EAST MOOR

BEELEY

PUB 22

BEELEY BROOK

RIVER DERWENT

B6012

QUARRY (Dis)

FB

BURNT WOOD

SMELTINGMILL WOOD

343M

ROWSLEY

PUBS 23, 24

DISMANTLED RAILWAY

A6

MILL

WOODSIDE

RIVER WYE

A6

CHESTERFIELD LANE

SMELTINGMILL BROOK

200M

300M

200M

300M

200M

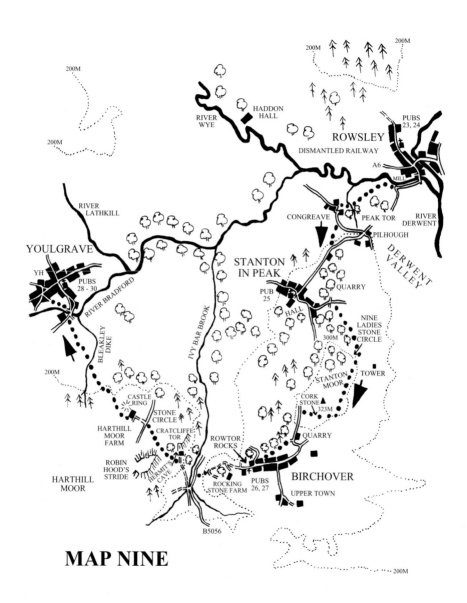

MAP NINE

CHATSWORTH PARK is a vast swathe of parkland that extends for 1,000 acres from Baslow to One Arch Bridge near Beeley. It straddles the banks of the River Derwent at the heart of which stands the magnificent Chatsworth House, affectionately known as the Palace of the Peak and home of the Duke of Devonshire. Chatsworth Park once formed the western edge of Sherwood Forest, although the present park was largely created by the 4th Duke during the mid 18th Century with the help of Lancelot 'Capability' Brown, England's greatest landscape gardener. The shape of the woods and plantations that trace the crests and contours of the hills are characteristic of his work, as are the numerous stands of trees within the park. Deer, cattle and sheep still roam across the unenclosed acres and there are ancient oak trees that have been growing for at least 1,000 years and boast a girth of almost 30 feet - perhaps Robin Hood hid in some of these trees? *"On the farther bank roam herds of red and fallow deer - the former descendants of those that ran wild in the forgotten Forest of the Peak. On a misty day, when house and bridge, and bower are all veiled, these magnificent animals have a most impressive appearance - they move slowly then - there are no wild flights - they scorn man and are lords of the whole park."* **(R. Murray Gilchrist, 'The Peak District', 1911).** The Chatsworth Estate stretches far beyond Chatsworth Park covering some 35,000 acres of land that includes estate villages, grouse moors, woodland, quarries, rivers and working farms. For many years, successive Dukes have taken a very enlightened approach to access and allowed people to wander freely across Chatsworth Park, which gives the area an enhanced sense of space and freedom.

CHATSWORTH HOUSE is one of the finest and most famous stately homes in England, the epitome of the English country house that has been the home of the Cavendish family, the Dukes of Devonshire, for over 450 years. In 1549, Bess of Hardwick and her second husband Sir William Cavendish, a wealthy aristocrat who made his fortune during Henry VIII's Dissolution of the Monasteries, bought the manor of Chatsworth and subsequently began to build a mansion house that took many years to complete; their son William became the 1st Earl of Devonshire in 1618. The only buildings to still survive from this period are the Hunting Tower that rises above the wooded escarpment of Stand

Wood above Chatsworth House from where ladies could follow the progress of a hunting party below, and also Queen Mary's Bower that stands near Chatsworth Bridge. This is a rare survivor of the original Tudor buildings that is named after Mary Queen of Scots who was held captive at Chatsworth during the 16th Century. This unusual building is said to stand on the site of an ancient earthwork that once protected a ford across the river.

The present Palladian-style house was a rebuilding, wing by wing, of the Tudor mansion house executed between 1686 and 1707 by the 4th Earl, who became the 1st Duke of Devonshire in 1694 for his part in bringing William of Orange to the throne. The layout of Chatsworth Park and the landscape that surrounds the house are largely the creation of the 4th Duke during the mid 18th Century, a prominent Whig politician who served as Prime Minister during the 1750s. He employed James Paine, a famous Georgian architect, to build the stable block (1763) and Chatsworth Bridge (1762) across the River Derwent as well as new approach roads to the house. The 4th Duke then employed 'Capability' Brown to landscape the park and gardens to give them a more 'natural' feel popular at that time. Brown also altered the course of the river, enclosed what was to become Chatsworth Park and had the houses of the original Edensor village razed to the ground as they spoilt the Duke's view from his house! Favourable marriages coupled with revenues from their extensive lands and mining interests during the late 18th and early 19th Centuries meant that the Cavendish family became extremely wealthy with extensive lands throughout England and Ireland, during which time they accrued a vast collection of art treasures. During the 19th Century the 6th Duke employed Joseph Paxton as head gardener who transformed the formal gardens with the addition of the Emperor Fountain with its 280-ft gravity-fed plume of water as well as the now-demolished Great Conservatory - the forerunner of the Crystal Palace which Paxton designed for the Great Exhibition of 1851. During the 20th Century, onerous death duties meant that many art treasures, properties and land had to be sold including Devonshire House in Piccadilly and Hardwick Hall with its associated farms and land, which went to the National Trust. The ownership of all the remaining

Derbyshire estates then passed to the Trustees of the Chatsworth Settlement, but the central parts of the estate, most used by visitors, including the house, garden and park, are now leased to the Chatsworth House Trust, an independent charity, to ensure their long term survival. It is still the family home of the Duke and Duchess of Devonshire, with the 12th Duke now in residence. A tour of Chatsworth House and gardens is a must to see one of Europe's finest private art collections built up over almost five centuries (and still growing) by the Cavendish family, much of which is displayed in the sumptuously painted and decorated rooms and halls throughout the house that also includes one of the world's greatest private libraries. *"Almost everything pertaining to Chatsworth, both inside and outside, is splendid and magnificent, and it will save visitors the vexation of having these words constantly before their eyes, if they will kindly realise this fact to begin with, and excuse us for not repeating them with each work of art to which we shall draw passing attention."* **(M. J. B. Baddeley, 'The Peak District of Derbyshire and Neighbouring Counties', 1887).**

The One Arch Bridge and derelict Chatsworth Mill can be found at the southern end of the park, both of which were designed by James Paine during the 1760s. This mill worked until 1952 grinding corn for animal feed, but was partly destroyed during a gale in 1962.

Chatsworth House

EDENSOR, pronounced Ensor, is undoubtedly the finest of the Chatsworth Estate villages with the spire of St Peter's Church pointing towards the heavens surrounded by a cluster of houses each with their own unique architectural style. The original village spread nearer to the river but much of it was pulled down by the 4th Duke and it was not until 1838 that the 6th Duke began to rebuild the village around its church. Along with Joseph Paxton, the Duke commissioned a young architect from Derby called John Robertson to come up with designs. It was quite usual back then to prepare a portfolio of various designs to choose from but apparently the Duke liked them all, which explains the eclectic architecture ranging from mock-Tudor to Italian and Swiss style houses. This architectural anarchy actually works extremely well thanks largely to the use of warm honey-coloured sandstone throughout as well as the blue Chatsworth livery paintwork on the fascias and drainpipes that give the buildings a sense of unity. All that remains of the original village high street is the solitary Park Cottage hidden amidst the undulating parkland, saved because it was not visible form the house. The focal point is St Peter's Church, built in 1869 on the site of the original 14th Century church by renowned architect Sir George Gilbert Scott. The church boasts many interesting features including the rather macabre monument to Bess of Hardwick's two sons and the tomb of Lord Frederick Cavendish who, as Chief Secretary for Ireland in Gladstone's government, arrived in Dublin with a message of peace but was infamously murdered in Pheonix Park, Dublin in 1882 by Irish nationalist group The Invincibles. Look for the wreath of everlasting flowers sent by Queen Victoria for Lord Frederick's funeral. In the churchyard are several Cavendish graves, whilst of particular note is the grave of Kathleen Kennedy who lies buried beside the dukes. She was the widow of William Cavendish, the Marquess of Hartington and eldest son of the 10th Duke, and daughter of Joseph Kennedy, Ambassador of the United States to Great Britain. She died in a plane crash in 1948 aged just 28, four years after her husband had been killed in action during the Second World War whilst serving with the Coldstream Guards. Her brother, John F. Kennedy, visited her grave five months before his assassination. Sir Joseph Paxton also lies buried in this churchyard.

BEELEY has been an estate village of the Dukes of Devonshire since the mid 18th Century when most of it was purchased as part of the 'grand plan' to redevelop Chatsworth Park. The history of the village stretches much further back to pre-Conquest times when it formed part of a small manor held by a Saxon chieftain. The oldest building is St Anne's Church, which dates back to Norman times although only fragments remain of this early church as it was heavily restored in the 1880s. Of particular note is the fine Norman doorway with an unusual carved head above the door, whilst inside is a bassoon that dates from around 1750 when it was used for church music before the organ was installed. There is a large and ancient yew tree in the churchyard held together by chains that is thought to be older than the church itself, which may indicate a pagan religious site. Yew trees had great religious significance in ancient times and were regarded as the symbolic 'tree of life' and were often planted on sacred pagan ground before being adopted by the early Christian church for their church sites. Our Celtic ancestors had uncanny foresight when they named the yew 'tree of life' for currently taxol, a chemical present in their leaves and bark, is used as a treatment for certain forms of cancer - but do not try eating the leaves as they are highly poisonous! The strong, flexible wood was prized in medieval times as the finest wood for longbows.

The original village developed around the church, where the former village green can be still be seen just to the east of the churchyard. Many of the houses throughout the village date from a building spree during the 19th Century by the 6th Duke including the school, chapel, reading room and several cottages, however, a number of older properties remain including the 17th Century Old Hall and the 18th Century Devonshire Arms. This classic Peakland pub was once a coaching inn that welcomed many famous customers including Charles Dickens and King Edward VII, who supposedly met his mistress Alice Keppel here! During 2006, this pub came back under Chatsworth Estate management as part of their exclusive Devonshire Hotels group and, after a major refurbishment, cleverly combines a modern bistro and contemporary bedrooms with a traditional village pub. Although a number of properties are now privately owned, the Chatsworth influence remains strong with its blue livery in evidence.

To the south of Beeley lies Burnt Wood and Smeltingmill Wood, a delightful swathe of woodland with a dramatic boulder-strewn wooded ravine. As these names suggest, there was a small lead smelting mill here that was in use during the 17th Century but probably dates back much further, built here because of the plentiful supply of timber to fire the hearths and also the steep ground to assist the flues. Lead mining and smelting in the Peak District can be traced back to Roman times, although the lead mining heyday was between the 17th and early 19th Centuries when the area was one of the largest ore-fields in the world. The lead mining industry finally came to an end during the early years of the 20th Century due to dwindling reserves and cheaper imports. Hidden away in the heart of this woodland beside Smeltingmill Brook are the spoil heaps and workings of a quarry that produced high quality building stone. The spoil heaps are now covered with moss and the workings are slowly being reclaimed by nature but the scale of the quarry is quite impressive with its large retaining wall and spoil heaps piled up high above the tumbling stream.

ROWSLEY is situated at the confluence of the rivers Wye and Derwent on the edge of the National Park boundary. It also lies at the cusp of two dukedoms, although it falls within the bounds of the Duke of Rutland's estate (the Manners family) of nearby Haddon Hall, probably the finest medieval manor house in England that lies just over a mile to the west towards Bakewell. It is a village divided in two by the River Derwent, which is spanned by a 15th Century packhorse bridge that has been widened several times to cope with the incessant traffic that speeds on its way to Bakewell and beyond. The settlement on the eastern riverbank, once known as Little Rowsley, largely developed following the arrival of the Midland Railway's line from Derby in 1849. The railway terminated at Rowsley until 1863 because the route between here and Manchester was challenged by the Duke of Devonshire who did not want it to cross Chatsworth Park. An alternative route was found up through the Wye Valley across the Duke of Rutland's estate on condition that it was concealed in deep cuttings and tunnels as it passed Haddon Hall. The only problem with this new route was that the original Rowsley Station, a fine Italianate building designed by Joseph

Paxton, was now sited in the wrong place as it had been built for the proposed Derwent Valley route. Paxton's station was left marooned and demoted to use as sidings and yards whilst a new station was built just to the south. When the railway closed in 1968 between Matlock and Buxton the old railway yards were redeveloped as the Peak Village shopping centre with Paxton's station as its centrepiece. Reminders of this once busy railway centre are everywhere with an impressive stone-built viaduct across the River Derwent, railway workers' cottages and the Grouse and Claret pub, formerly the Station Hotel. To the west of the riverbank lies Great Rowsley, the original settlement that boasts a real village atmosphere with its water fountain, lamp standard dated 'VR 1887', several 17th and 18th Century farms and cottages as well as St Katherine's Church that is noted for the tomb of Lady Catherine Manners, first wife of the 7th Duke of Rutland who died in 1859. The most impressive building is the Peacock, built in 1652 as a yeoman's house on land leased from the Manners family, whose crest features a peacock. For a time the building was used as the dower house of Haddon Hall but has been an inn since the 1820s. Around fifty years ago the hotel was sold by the Manners family but has recently been bought back by Lord Edward Manners of Haddon Hall (the Duke of Rutland's younger brother) who has overseen its transformation into a chic hotel. The Manners family have held the manor of Rowsley for many centuries and have provided the village with many notable buildings including the church and school. *"Here is the Peacock Hotel, a fine old Elizabethan hostelry with a lawn sloping to the Derwent. Some years ago the writer, staying at this inn with a party of ladies and gentlemen, asked for the day's paper in the smoke room. The reply was that the papers were not allowed to be taken out of the bar-parlour. Next morning a little after 8 o'clock, two of the party, being about to bathe in the Wye, asked for glasses of rum and milk. "The bar" was "not open," the servant said: a polite message was sent up-stairs to the landlady whose answer, as reported, was that the bar was "never opened till 9 o'clock." - The same name still appears on the signboard."* (**M. J. B. Baddeley, 1887).**

One of Rowsley's most historic buildings is Caudwell's Mill, which can be found at the bottom of School Lane near the River Wye. There has been a watermill on this site for many centuries, taking advantage of a mill race that loops from a meander along the fast-flowing Wye. The present stone-built mill complex was built by John Caudwell in 1874 and continued as a family business until 1978. Originally it had two waterwheels that powered millstones to grind wheat and grain, but these antiquated millstones produced grey bread flour and so were superseded by a revolutionary roller milling system in 1885 that produced white flour. To provide the necessary power, a water turbine was installed to replace one of the waterwheels in 1887 and then the second waterwheel was replaced in 1898 with a turbine that is still in use today. The mill flourished for many decades, indeed, at one time Caudwell's Flour was a well-known brand throughout Derbyshire. The mill is now operated by the Caudwell's Mill Trust and is a fascinating place to visit to see the flour being produced using original machinery. The mill also houses a café, craft workshops and shop and stands as the only complete Victorian water turbine powered roller mill in the country.

Rowsley

STANTON IN PEAK is an attractive hillside village situated on the north-western flanks of Stanton Moor with rather stark gritstone houses lining the sloping main street and lots of narrow lanes leading off.

"Stanton is a picturesque little hamlet - village it can hardly be called, for it is too insignificant in size - consisting of a few rustic cottages scattered promiscuously over the hillside, or built in tiers one above the other, with their gables abutting upon the way. The dwellings, though small, have a cleanly appearance outside, and here and there through the open doors you may see that there are not wanting signs of homely comfort and contentment within." **(James Croston, 'On Foot through The Peak', 1889).** The tower and spire of Holy Trinity Church dominate the skyline, its blue clock face a distinctive feature. Stanton is essentially an estate village of Stanton Hall, home of the Thornhill family since the late 17th Century - look out for the initials WPT on some of the buildings that refer to William Pole Thornhill who rebuilt parts of the village in the 1830s, including the church. At the heart of the village is the Flying Childers pub, named after a famous winning racehorse that belonged to the 4th Duke of Devonshire during the 18th Century. This classic Peakland pub remains totally unspoilt with a traditional bar complete with wooden settles, beamed ceiling and a coal fire. Opposite the pub stands Holly House, a fine three-storey early Georgian house that still has two blocked-up windows, a result of the 1697 Windows Tax although until recently a further six windows were also blocked up.

STANTON MOOR is a magical swathe of moorland carpeted with heather and dotted with sparse birch woodland, an outpost of the Dark Peak set amidst the eastern edges of the limestone White Peak. Such an unusual and distinctive landscape was interpreted by our ancestors as an area that warranted special status. Indeed, this is one of the most important Bronze Age sites in England with over seventy burial mounds, numerous standing stones and stone circles as well as prehistoric farming remains and house sites. The finest of these is the Nine Ladies Stone Circle, set in clearing just above the steep escarpment overlooking the Derwent Valley. This stone circle was built around 4,000 years ago and was originally surrounded by an earthen bank. Its purpose remains unknown, although rituals and ceremonies certainly took place here associated with the solstices, seasons and fertility. It is a very atmospheric place, especially in the depths of winter when the low afternoon sun slants through the birch trees. According to legend, the

Nine Ladies were turned to stone for dancing on the Sabbath, whilst the King Stone was the fiddler - the King Stone is a small outlier situated about 40 yards to the west. Such stories have often been attributed to stone circles as a way of Christianising a pagan religious site, thus trivialising Bronze Age culture. Nearby is the Earl Grey Tower, built in 1832 by the Thornhill family of Stanton Hall to commemorate the passing of the Reform Bill that both extended voting rights and altered parliamentary constituencies, which helped create the electoral system we have today.

During the early 20th Century father and son team J.C. and J.P. Heathcote of Birchover excavated many of the burial mounds across Stanton Moor and displayed their extensive finds in a small museum they set up in the village, later moved to the Sheffield Weston Park Museum. The wide path that leads across the moor affords wonderful views down the Derwent Valley towards Matlock, whilst beside the path are excavated burial mounds and cairns. The southern end of Stanton Moor is marked by the Cork Stone, a solitary mushroom-shaped outcrop of sandstone with foot-holes and hand-grips that allow a rather precarious ascent of this rock. It is a natural outcrop of rock, although some historians believe it may have formed part of a large stone circle. What is certain, however, is that such a striking feature would have only enhanced our ancestors' perception that this area was indeed a very special place. Nearby is a large working stone quarry. Stone has been quarried from this moorland for many centuries as the rock is of an exceptional quality that is prized as a building stone for detailed work such as lintels.

BIRCHOVER is situated on a sloping hillside just below Stanton Moor, its grey-stone houses lining a long main street. The name of the village means 'birch covered slope' and was mentioned in the Domesday Book, although the site of the original settlement is thought to have been slightly to the south at what is now rather grandly known as Upper Town but which is, in reality, a handful of farms and cottages. Again, it is the rocks that draw visitors to Birchover. Behind the Druid Inn stand the Rowtor Rocks, a weird and wonderful collection of gritstone outcrops carved and fashioned into fantastic shapes by nature and man. A maze of steps, caves, passageways, seats, rooms and a three-seater armchair have been carved out of solid rock. According to local legend, these rock cuttings were made by Druids thousands of years ago as a temple and sacrificial altar, although they were most probably made by the local vicar Thomas Eyre in the early 18th Century when he built an eccentric study for himself from where he could admire the view whilst planning his sermons! These stories of Druids and their sacrificial altars became popular during Georgian and Victorian times and have never really disappeared, probably because we would all like the stories to be true. In reality, truth and myth are closely intertwined for there are several prehistoric carvings including cup and ring marked rocks across the outcrops, which adds weight to the theory that this indeed was a religious pagan site. The Reverend Eyre also built a small chapel along the lane just down from the Druid Inn in about 1700. The name of the rocks comes from two large 'rocking stones' to be found amongst the maze of rocks and crevices - great care must be taken if exploring these rocks as there are sheer drops and hidden hollows.

HARTHILL MOOR is perhaps even more enigmatic than Stanton Moor, indeed the whole swathe of land between Youlgrave and Birchover is a mystical landscape littered with relics from a forgotten age. There is an atmosphere that hangs heavy in the air, a feeling that you are amongst something very special and old; a sense that you are not alone. The Portway track-way, that ancient Iron Age route which linked important cultural and spiritual sites throughout the Peak District, cuts across Harthill Moor passing Robin Hood's Stride and Castle Ring hill-fort - our route follows this ancient highway from the main road below Birchover to Harthill Moor Farm. The most striking feature is Robin Hood's Stride, a large outcrop of gritstone rocks that dominates Harthill Moor. It is often referred to as Mock Beggar Hall due to its two slender gritstone pinnacles that rise up like the chimneys of a great house. Seen from a distance at dusk and silhouetted against the sky, it is easy to see how weary travellers' hearts may have lifted upon seeing what they thought to be a great hall in the vain hope of rest and refreshment. The two pinnacles are known by rock-climbers as Weasel and Inaccessible - the outcrops are named after the famed outlaw who reputedly jumped from one pinnacle to another to evade capture. *"The stride which Robin*

Hood must have taken to get the place named after him – i.e. the distance from turret to turret – is perhaps 10 to 15 yards. We have already seen that 'Little' John, by the measurement of his grave at Hathersage, was 10 feet high – so putting the two facts together, we have incontestable evidence that 'there were giants in those days'. **(M. J. B. Baddeley, 1887).**

Just to the east of Robin Hood's Stride hidden amongst trees at the foot of Cratcliff Tor is the Hermit's Cave. This small cave was certainly occupied by a hermit during the 16th Century as it is mentioned in the records of Haddon Hall. He would have helped and preached to travellers along the Portway. Historians believe that this cave is much older and that the stone carving of Jesus and the lamp recess are actually 700 years old. It is a truly spiritual place that lies hidden, dark and secretive, behind an ancient yew tree. Just to the north of Robin Hood's Stride is the Nine Stones (or Nine Stone Close) stone circle, although only four remain standing. It is believed that this stone circle stands in alignment with the rock formations of Robin Hood's Stride when, during the summer solstice, the full moon hangs low in the sky and passes between the two pinnacles. When complete, this stone circle would have been quite impressive as they are the largest standing stones in Derbyshire. To add more mystery to this landscape, just to the north of Harthill Moor Farm (and just off our footpath) is a large Iron Age hill-fort known as Castle Ring that occupies a promontory of land.

BRADFORD DALE is a beautiful limestone valley with steep slopes rising up to the houses of Youlgrave and a series of small weirs along the river to provide good fishing. This valley provides a tantalising taste of things to come as you leave the Dark Peak behind with its broad valleys, jagged escarpments and heather moorland and enter the wonderful world of the White Peak. This is a rich and varied landscape that is characterised by a high limestone plateau criss-crossed by drystone walls where you will find attractive villages, cosy pubs and a fascinating industrial heritage from lead mines to some of England's earliest mills. This plateau is dissected by steep-sided valleys cloaked in ancient woodland through which flow crystal-clear streams. This White Peak landscape will keep you company until Eyam, a day and a half's walking away.

YOULGRAVE is pronounced Youlgrave, the road-sign into the village says Youlgrave yet most guidebooks say Youlgreave. To add to this confusion, Ordnance Survey have recently changed their minds and altered the name on the most up-to-date Explorer map from Youlgreave to Youlgrave. In fact, local historians have found over 50 variations of the name recorded throughout the centuries. The name is probably derived from 'yellow groove' as the word 'groove' is a local term for a lead mine - this was once an important centre for lead mining. Just to confuse matters even more, the village is known locally as Pommie! This nickname is said to have originated long ago when the village brass (now silver) band was first established and only a handful of members knew how to play their horns. So off they went marching down the main street playing more of a 'pom, pom' sound rather than a recognisable tune!

This linear village straddles a spur of land between the limestone valleys of Lathkill Dale and Bradford Dale - it stretches three-quarters of a mile from end to end. Perhaps what most people remember about Youlgrave is its very narrow main street where buses and cars squeeze past each other and, in places, there is not even room for a pavement. Amongst the old cottages and clutch of traditional shops and inns that line this main street are several notable buildings including The Old Hall of 1656 that overlooks the top of Holywell Lane, a fine stone-built house that is all gables and mullions. The ghosts of a Roundhead and Cavalier are said to haunt this hall, locked in an endless duel from the English Civil War. Behind this Old Hall is another fine 17th Century hall known as Old Hall Farm. In the heart of the village overlooking the Fountain is Thimble Hall, the smallest detached house in the world. This tiny one-up-one-down 18th Century house has only two rooms measuring 8-ft by 7-ft that are connected by a ladder. Amazingly, this building once housed a family of eight and was last used as a house in the 1930s. The Youth Hostel also overlooks Fountain Square, housed in the former Co-Operative Stores that was built in 1887 and still retains its ornate Victorian frontage. The Fountain is the focal point of the village, a circular stone water storage tank that was built in 1829 by a group of local women known as the 'Friendly Society of Women' who came together to demand a clean water supply to replace the waters of the River Bradford. The water was piped from a spring near Mawstone Mine to the south of Youlgrave and then stored in the Fountain, which has a capacity of 1,500 gallons. Villagers were then charged sixpence a year to use the water. Clean water was cause for great celebration, so much so that the villagers revived the ancient Well Dressing ceremony. Each June, the Fountain and five other old wells throughout the village are 'dressed' with pictorial flower displays, one of the best in the Peak District. Over thirty villages throughout the Peak District have well dressings during the summer. This custom has its origins in pagan times when people worshipped a constant and pure supply of water, especially in the White Peak where the pervious limestone bedrock means that streams are few and far between. As Christianity replaced pagan worship, many of the ancient traditions were simply given new Christian meaning. Over the centuries, well dressings have progressed from simple offerings to lavish floral displays where petals and other natural materials are mounted on boards of clay to create vivid pictorial scenes, predominantly Biblical. Along with Youlgrave, some of the more famous well dressings take place at Tissington, Tideswell, Litton and Ashford.

All Saints Church dominates the village, its magnificent Perpendicular bell tower rising almost 100-ft above the rooftops calling the faithful to prayer from the surrounding villages as it has done for over 500 years. The present building dates back to the mid 12th Century, although it stands on a religious site used since Saxon times. The spacious nave is predominately Norman with lovely arcades and pillars capped by finely carved capitals, whilst the rest of the church dates from the 14th and 15th Centuries. Inside, look out for the magnificent tomb of a 13th Century knight believed to be Sir John Rossington whilst nearby is the 15th Century alabaster tomb of Thomas Cockayne dressed in armour, who lived a nearby Harthill Hall. This tomb is unusually small because he predeceased his father. Also of note is the unique Norman font that has a small stoop for holy water attached to the main font by means of a carved salamander, the symbol of baptism. Nearby is a small 12th Century figure of a pilgrim carved into the wall at the western end of the nave, one of the most intriguing features of this church. Once you have pondered this pilgrim's purpose, look westwards along the nave to the fine East Window, the work of Pre-Raphaelite painter Edward Burne-Jones who produced it in the workshops of William Morris.

YOULGRAVE
to
TIDESWELL

✦

"The limestone valleys of the White Peak are the crowning glory of the Peak District, hidden gardens of Eden where nature abounds and beauty triumphs. Lathkill Dale is amongst the finest, a wonderful world of crystal-clear streams, ancient woodland, towering crags and steep slopes with the sound of birdsong and sweet smell of wild flowers and herbs all around. Visit in late spring and the greensward slopes of the upper valley are carpeted with swathes of cowslip, orchid and Jacob's ladder that bring vivid colour to the hillside and richness to your mind's-eye that no amount of grey weather can erase. But note; these secretive valleys do not present their riches willingly for you must walk through them to discover them."

Mark Reid
May 2006

WALK INFORMATION

Points of interest:	Seven dales in a day, a sparkling river, National Nature Reserves, flooded lead mines, ancient woodland, limestone caves and cliffs, Peakland's most famous viewpoint, the valley of the gods, full steam ahead, dark satanic mills and a rather jolly end to the walk.

Distance:

Youlgrave to Monyash	6 miles
Monyash to Monsal Head	5.75 miles
Monsal Head to Tideswell	4.25 miles
Total	16 miles

Time: Allow 7 - 8 hours

Terrain: Between Youlgrave and Monyash, this walk follows clear paths through Bradford Dale and Lathkill Dale alongside rivers, through woodland and across rough limestone terrain. From Monyash, a country lane and then field paths lead across the White Peak plateau passing Magpie Mine (ruins) to reach Sheldon. From Sheldon, a track and then field paths lead over into Deep Dale with a steep descent along a rough path into this wooded valley. A wide path then leads up through Monsal Dale alongside the River Wye before slanting up across the steep wooded hillside (steep drops) to Monsal Head. The walk then follows the Monsal Trail (old railway line) up through the valley to reach Cressbrook Tunnel where a path cuts across a steep hillside to Cressbrook Mill. A permissive path then heads up through Water-cum-Jolly Dale alongside the River Wye (liable to flooding) to reach

Litton Mill from where a path heads up through Tideswell Dale to Tideswell.

Expect muddy or flooded conditions after rain in all of the valleys. Do not explore the old mine workings and keep to the path through Lathkill Dale and around Magpie Mine – hidden shafts. Limestone is slippery when wet. Take care crossing the A6 at White Lodge.

Permissive Paths:

The path through Lathkill Dale National Nature Reserve between Lathkill Lodge and Carter's Mill is a permissive path that is closed on Wednesdays from October to January. An alternative route has been given within the Route Description.

The path from Monsal Head to Litton Mill follows the Monsal Trail along the old railway track-bed with a permissive path around the blocked-up Cressbrook Tunnel via Water-cum-Jolly Dale. If this path is no longer available or flooded, then an alternative route has been given within the Route Description.

Ascents:

Magpie Mine:	335 metres
Monsal Head:	235 metres

Viewpoints:

Lathkill Dale from above Conksbury Bridge.
Upper Lathkill Dale from Ricklow Quarry.
White Peak plateau from Magpie Mine.
Views across Monsal Dale from descent into Deep Dale.
Looking across Monsal Dale from Monsal Head.
Cressbrook Mill from the Monsal Trail.

FACILITIES

Youlgrave	Inn / B&B / Shop / PO / Bus / Phone / Toilets / YH / Camp
Alport	Bus / Phone
Monyash	Inn / B&B / Café / Bus / Phone / Toilets / Camp
Sheldon	Inn / Bus / Phone
White Lodge	Bus / Toilets
Monsal Head	Inn / B&B / Café / Bus / Toilets / Camp
Cressbrook Mill	Café
Tideswell Dale	Bus / Toilets
Tideswell	Inn / B&B / Shop / PO / Café / Bus / Phone / Toilets / YH

ROUTE DESCRIPTION

(Map Ten)

From The Fountain in the centre of Youlgrave, head along the Main Street to reach All Saints Church. Turn right along the lane immediately before the church (Bradford Road leading to Mawstone Lane) and follow this down heading out of the village then, just before the last house on your left (Braemar House), bear off to the left along an enclosed path passing behind Braemar House down to reach a packhorse bridge across the River Bradford. Cross the bridge and follow the wide gravel track to the left heading down through the valley (River Bradford to your left) then, where this track bends up to the right, head straight on off the track and through a kissing-gate. Follow the path straight on across a field (river just across to your left) to soon re-join the river again, which you follow downstream passing the limestone outcrop of Rhienstor to reach a gate across the track on the outskirts of Alport. Head through the gate, over a bridge across the River Bradford and straight on to join the main road beside a bridge across the River Lathkill.

At the road take the FP opposite through a squeeze-stile beside a gate (SP 'Conksbury') and follow the path straight on across the field (ignore track behind the buildings) to reach a gate in the far corner (River Lathkill on your right). A clear path now heads straight on alongside a wall on your right across several fields and through a series of squeeze-stiles (River Lathkill just across to your right) for just over 0.5 miles to reach a lane just below Raper Lodge. At the lane, carry straight on along the rough track opposite (SP 'Lathkill Dale') and follow this straight on with woodland on your right then, where this woodland ends and the track bends to the right into a field, head straight on through a small gate in a fence. Follow the path ahead to reach a road where you turn right down to reach Conksbury Bridge across the River Lathkill.

Cross Conksbury Bridge, a short distance after which take the turning to the left (SP) through a gate and follow the wide path down through woodland to join the banks of the River Lathkill. Carry straight on along this clear path heading up through the valley (river to your left) passing a series of weirs and small lakes. After 0.5 miles you reach a small gate in a wall (just above the last weir), after which carry straight on across the wooded hillside then down across a short section of rocky limestone to join the wooded riverbank (river now follows a natural course rather than artificial lakes). Follow this riverside path to soon reach a clapper bridge and ford across the river beside Lathkill Lodge. *(Alternative route between Lathkill Lodge and Carter's Mill from this point - see Alternative Routes below)*.

Turn right up along the lane for a few paces then left along a stony track skirting around the old mill building to reach a gate on the edge of the National Nature Reserve *(permissive path through the Nature Reserve)*. Head through the gate and follow the track straight on heading up through wooded Lathkill Dale, with the river to your left. After just under 0.5 miles you pass between two old stone gateposts and enter woodland, with the Mandale Mine drainage sough beside the track to your left *(Mandale Mine Engine House just up to your right in the woodland)*. Continue straight on along the wide track through the woodland (river still on your left) passing the stone-built supports of the old aqueduct, after which carry on along the clear track heading up through the wooded valley to soon reach a wooden FB across the river that leads to Bateman's House just across the river (lead mine ruins). After visiting the ruins, continue along the clear track heading up through Palmerston Wood with the River Lathkill on your left for about 0.75 miles to reach a gate at the end of Palmerston Wood/Nature Reserve just beyond a weir/large pond. Head through the gate and walk straight on to quickly reach another gate (track ends), after which follow the riverside path straight on passing the ruins of Carter's mill (two millstones) with a weir and Carter's mill pond on your left.

(Map Eleven)

Carry straight on along the clear riverside path with Carter's mill pond on your left heading up through steep-sided Lathkill Dale. Just beyond the mill pond you pass Lathkill Falls (path becomes rougher underfoot) where you carry on through sparse woodland to soon reach a wall-stile across your path. Cross the stile and follow the stony path heading up through the valley along the wooded riverbank for about 0.5 miles to reach a crossroads of paths beside a FB (valley opens out - woodland left behind). Do not cross this FB but continue along the narrow path alongside the river on your left heading up along the valley floor. You soon pass the summer source of the river, beyond which the riverbed is often dry - continue along the narrow path heading up through the valley alongside a wall on your left following the valley as it gently curves round to the left. Where the wall ends with Lathkill Head Cave just to your left *(winter source of the river)* carry on along the narrow, rocky path heading up through the dry limestone valley to reach a wall-stile towards the head of the valley. Cross the stile and follow the rough path up over boulders *(old workings of Ricklow Quarry)* through a narrow limestone valley for 0.25 miles to reach a kissing-gate across your path at the head of Lathkill Dale (valley opens out). Head through the kissing-gate and follow the broad grassy path up through the shallow valley to reach the B5055 on the outskirts of Monyash.

Turn left up along the road into Monyash to reach the green in the centre of the village. As you reach the top of the green (just after the pub), turn right at the crossroads towards 'Flagg, Sheldon' along Chapel Street and follow this heading out of Monyash. As you reach the edge of the village the road drops down a small bank, at the bottom of which take the turning to the right towards 'Sheldon'. Follow this road gently rising up for 0.5 miles passing the turning towards Nursery Fields Farm, 200 yards after which take the FP to the left through a squeeze-stile (SP). Head to the right diagonally across the field to a wall-stile beside a gate in the top right corner, after which head straight on keeping fairly close to the wall on your right to reach a wall-stile across your path just up from the bottom corner of the field. Cross this stile and walk straight on over a tumbledown wall then on to reach another wall-stile in the bottom corner of the field (line of old workings just beyond wall). After this wall-stile, bear slightly left up to reach a wall-stile beside a gate in the top left corner, after which head straight on alongside the wall on your left across the top of three fields to reach a belt of woodland across your path (Hard Rake Plantation). As you approach this woodland (end of the third field), bear slightly right cutting off the corner of the field to reach a wall-stile, after which head straight on across the narrow 'triangular' field corner and over another wall-stile that leads into the woodland. Head straight on through the woodland and over a wall-stile that leads back out onto a field where you head straight on alongside the wall on your right to reach a road. Turn right along the road (ignore road turning to the left after a short distance) and follow the road bending down to the right into a shallow 'dip', at the bottom of which (250 yards after the turning) turn left over a wall-stile beside a gate. Follow the rough track straight on passing through a gap in a tumbledown wall (just after a dew pond), after which head straight on across the field (heading towards the left-side of Magpie Mine ahead) to reach a large wall-gap in the top left field corner. After this large wall-gap turn left through another wall-gap then round to the right across the field and cross over the corner of a wall (jutting out into the field) then carry on to reach Magpie Mine.

Pass between the buildings (Engine House to your left) and follow the track straight on to quickly join another track across your path (former mine agent's house on your right). Turn left along this track then, where it forks after a few paces, follow the left-hand track bearing left again after a short distance passing the Engine House and chimney on your left then head away from the mine buildings bearing to the left across the rough field to join a wall on your left. Follow the grassy path alongside this wall across the rough field to reach a wall-stile in the top left corner. Cross this stile and bear slightly left across the field to reach a squeeze-stile in the field corner, after which carry straight on across the next field and through a small wall-gate that leads onto the top of a walled grassy track (SP). Head straight on across the grassy track through a squeeze-stile just ahead tucked away in the corner, after which head alongside the wall on your right then, where this wall bends to the right, cross the wall-stile to the right. After the wall-stile, head left across the middle of the field to reach a wall-stile in the far right field corner on the edge of Sheldon (SP), after which follow the path skirting to the right around the house gardens and through a gateway to the left of the house that leads onto the village green and road at the top end of Sheldon.

Turn right down along the road into the village passing the Cock & Pullet just after which turn left along a track (SP 'Sheldon Parish Church'). Follow this track passing the church after which the track curves round to the left then, where the walled track forks (and the stony track bends sharp right), carry straight on along the enclosed grassy track down to reach a gate across the track after 200 yards. Head straight on through the gate (ignore walled path to the right) and follow this enclosed track down for another 200 yards then, where it curves down to the right, take the FP to the left over a wall-stile (SP). After the wall-stile, head to the right across the field to quickly reach another wall-stile, after which head up across the field keeping close to the wall on your left to reach a wall-stile across your path slightly to the right from the top field corner. Cross this wall-stile and carry straight on across several fields over a succession of wall-stiles to reach an enclosed grassy path, which you follow straight on to soon reach the bottom of a walled grassy track where you turn right through a gate out onto a field (SP). Head straight on alongside the wall on your left, through a gateway in a field corner after which carry straight on for 100 yards then cross the wall-stile to the left (SP). After the stile, head straight down the field alongside the wall on your left then, about 100 yards before the bottom of the field (waymarker), head to the right down into a 'dip' to reach a wall-stile at the top of a steep wooded bank *(Deep Dale Nature Reserve)*. Cross the stile and follow the rough path steeply down the wooded hillside alongside a wall to reach a footpath across your path (halfway down the hillside). Turn left along the path (SP 'White Lodge car park') and follow it gradually dropping down across the steep wooded hillside to emerge from the woods into Deep Dale where you come to a junction of paths. Turn right (SP 'White Lodge car park, A6') and follow the path winding down to reach a wall-stile set amongst trees at the bottom of Deep Dale. Cross the stile and a stream just beyond, immediately after which turn right alongside the stream/wall at first then bearing round to the left (away from the stream/wall) across the hillside along a clear path to reach White Lodge car park.

Head straight on over the lane through the car park where you follow the path ahead to the left down steps to reach the A6. Cross the road *(take care - fast road)* and take the FP opposite through a squeeze-stile (SP), after which follow the path down to quickly reach a stile and some stepping stones across a side-stream that leads into woodland. After the stile/stepping stones follow the clear wide path ahead (ignore path up to the left after a short distance) heading up through Monsal Dale alongside the River Wye passing through woodland, across wooded pastures and along the riverbank for 1 mile to reach a FB across the river (just downstream of a large weir). Cross the FB and follow the path to the left to reach the weir where you follow the path to the right slanting gradually up across the steep wooded hillside to reach the road at the top of the steep bank at Monsal Head.

(Map Twelve)

(Alternative route from Monsal Head to Litton Mill from this point - see Alternative Routes below). As you reach the road at Monsal Head (at the top of the steep bank), head straight on along the footpath ahead (SP 'Upperdale, Monsal Viaduct') dropping steeply back down the hillside into Monsal Dale (stone steps) then, where the path forks after 100 yards, turn left (SP 'Viaduct & Monsal Trail') and follow the path slanting down across the wooded hillside to join the track-bed of the former Midland Railway line beside a blocked-up tunnel. Turn right along the track-bed (Monsal Trail) over Monsal Viaduct then continue straight on along the old track-bed for a further 0.75 miles (passing the former Monsal Dale Station) to reach a bridlegate to your right just before the blocked-up Cressbrook Tunnel. Head through the bridlegate and follow the path across the steep hillside with the River Wye down to your right (ignore narrow path branching up to the left) then passing above Cressbrook Mill just after which the path winds down rocky steps to the right to reach a FB above the river just below the weir and mill pond. Cross the FB and follow the path straight on for a short distance then, where it forks, head left over a FB across the mill race (SP 'Concession Path to Litton Mill'), with the mill pond on your left.

If the permissive path through Water-cum-Jolly Dale is flooded or no longer available, turn right at the fork in the path alongside the mill race and follow the enclosed path through the yard of Cressbrook Mill to join a road. Turn left along the road, forking immediately left then follow the alternative route from Cressbrook Mill to Litton Mill (see Alternative Routes below).

Follow the broad path straight on curving around the mill pond hugging sheer limestone outcrops on your right - continue along the wide path heading up through Water-cum-Jolly Dale alongside the still waters of the River Wye on your left following this sinuous, wooded valley for just over a mile to reach Litton Mill. As you reach the mill buildings, follow the track to the right across a bridge over the mill race then round to the left through the former mill yard (mill on your left) to reach the entrance gates to the mill. Head through the gates and carry straight on along the road passing a row of cottages on your right and continue along the road leaving Litton Mill behind (River Wye on your left) then, after 300 yards, take the track branching off to the right (SP 'Tideswell Dale'). Follow the wide path for 1 mile heading up through Tideswell Dale alongside the stream passing through woodland at first then across pastures (choice of paths either side of the stream) then back through woodland up to reach Tideswell Dale car park. Head straight on across the car park then, as you approach the entrance, follow the path ahead (on the right-hand side of the car park) lined by a row of large trees which leads up to soon join the road (B6049). Cross the road *(take care)* and turn right along the pavement for 250 yards passing the Water Treatment Works, immediately after which take the FP to the left through a small gate (SP). After the gate, head straight on up the hillside for a few paces then follow the path to the right slanting up across the hillside, through woodland then alongside a fence (path levels out) to reach a small gate to the left of a field gate that leads onto an enclosed track. Turn right along this track and follow it straight on, passing through a stonemason's yard then bearing right at the fork in the track to quickly join a road (Richard Lane) on the edge of Tideswell. Turn right down to join the main road where you turn left up into Tideswell

ALTERNATIVE ROUTES

Alternative route between Lathkill Lodge and Carter's Mill: As you reach the clapper bridge across the river beside Lathkill Lodge, turn right along the road and follow this steeply up into Over Haddon to reach a road junction beside a small triangular green in the village centre (car park to your left). Take the turning to the left passing the car park entrance up to quickly reach a T-junction where you turn left along the road out of the village. Follow this road straight on for 0.75 miles then take the turning off to the left and follow this for almost 0.75 miles to reach a track to the left, which you follow to reach Mill Farm. Where the track forks as you reach the farm buildings, bear left ahead (SP 'Lathkill Dale') passing between the barns to quickly reach a stile beside gate at the end of the farmyard that leads onto a grassy track. Follow this track curving to the right then gradually dropping down and bending to the left to reach a gate at the head of a small wooded side-valley. Head through the gate and follow the path straight on down along the left side of this valley. The path swings round to the left, through a gate then drops down into a larger side-valley, at the bottom of which follow the track bending sharp right then down through this valley to join the banks of the River Lathkill beside the ruins of Carter's mill (and Carter's mill pond). Turn right along the riverside path and follow the Route Description as from Map Eleven.

Alternative route between Monsal Head and Litton Mill (via Cressbrook Mill) if Monsal Trail or permissive path through Water-cum-Jolly Dale no longer available/flooded: As you reach the road at Monsal Head (at the top of the steep bank), head straight on along the footpath ahead (SP 'Upperdale, Monsal Viaduct') dropping steeply back down into Monsal Dale (stone steps) then, where the path forks after 100 yards, carry straight on (SP 'Monsal Dale') down across the wooded hillside to reach Netherdale Farm on your left at the bottom of the valley (path levels out). Carry straight on passing the buildings to soon reach a track on a sharp bend where you turn right to quickly join the road. Turn left and follow this road heading up through the valley, with the Wye to your left, passing the houses of Upperdale after 0.25 miles where you carry straight on along the road for a further 0.5 miles to reach Cressbrook Mill. Where the road forks just after Cressbrook Mill, take the left-hand fork and follow this climbing steeply up for almost 0.5 miles (ignore turnings off this road) to reach a road junction at the top of the climb. Turn left along the road and follow it bending round to the right then on passing Cressbrook Church just after which take the enclosed track branching off to the left (SP 'Litton Mill, Millers Dale'). Follow this track gradually dropping down to reach a gate at the end of the walled track, after which carry straight on along the grassy track heading down across the hillside to reach a gate in a fence. After the gate, follow the track to the left then bending sharp right (Litton Mill comes into view) and slanting down across the steep hillside before swinging down to the left into a grassy side-valley to reach a wall-stile beside a gate. After the wall-stile, follow the track straight on (becomes a lane) down into Litton Mill to reach the entrance gates to the mill. Turn right along the road and follow the Route Description as from Map Twelve (from Litton Mill).

Magpie Mine

146

MAP TEN

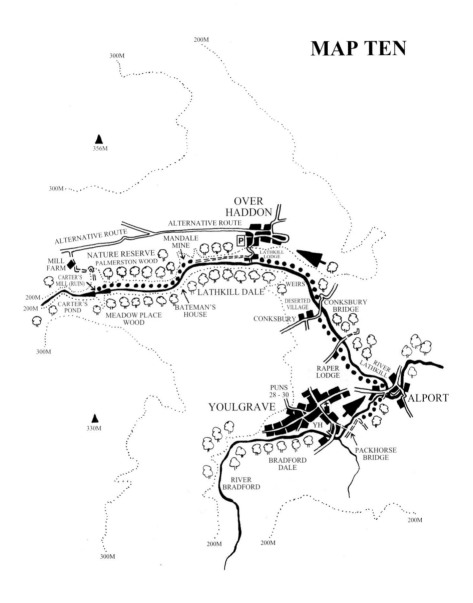

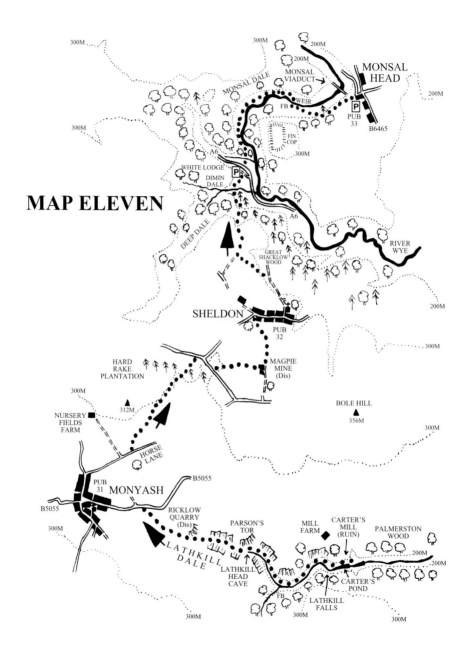

MAP ELEVEN

MONSAL HEAD

MONSAL VIADUCT

MONSAL DALE

WEIR

FB

PUB 33

B6465

FIN COP

A6

WHITE LODGE

DIMIN DALE

P

DEEP DALE

A6

GREAT SHACKLOW WOOD

RIVER WYE

200M
300M

SHELDON

PUB 32

HARD RAKE PLANTATION

MAGPIE MINE (Dis)

BOLE HILL
356M

312M

NURSERY FIELDS FARM

HORSE LANE

PUB 31 MONYASH

B5055

B5055

RICKLOW QUARRY (Dis)

PARSON'S TOR

MILL FARM

CARTER'S MILL (RUIN)

PALMERSTON WOOD

LATHKILL DALE

LATHKILL HEAD CAVE

CARTER'S POND

FB

LATHKILL FALLS

300M

300M

200M
200M

300M

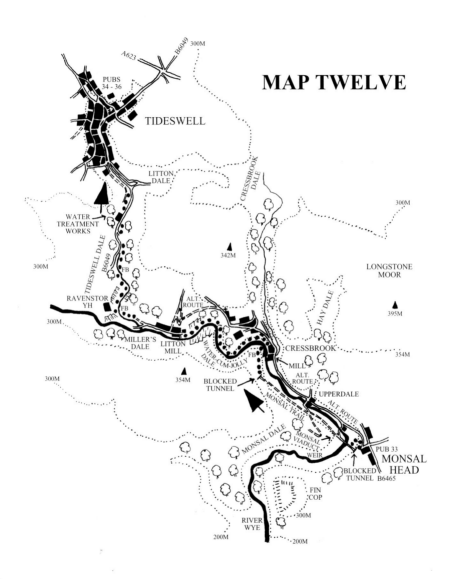

MAP TWELVE

PUBS 34 - 36

TIDESWELL

A623

B6049

300M

LITTON DALE

CRESSBROOK DALE

300M

WATER TREATMENT WORKS

342M

300M

LONGSTONE MOOR

TIDESWELL DALE

B6049

FB

HAY DALE

300M

395M

RAVENSTOR YH

ALT. ROUTE

FB

300M

MILLER'S DALE

LITTON MILL

WATER-CUM-JOLLY DALE

FB

CRESSBROOK

354M

354M

MILL

ALT. ROUTE

300M

BLOCKED TUNNEL

UPPERDALE

ALT. ROUTE

MONSAL TRAIL

MONSAL DALE

MONSAL VIADUCT

WEIR

PUB 33

MONSAL HEAD

BLOCKED TUNNEL

B6465

FIN COP

RIVER WYE

300M

200M

200M

ALPORT lies in a wooded hollow at the confluence of the rivers Bradford and Lathkill, a short but delightful walk from Youlgrave along a riverside path that crosses an old packhorse bridge before passing beneath limestone bluffs. Back in 1881 the River Bradford suddenly and mysteriously disappeared following heavy rain. The torrential downpours had opened an underground passageway that connected with the famous Hillcarr Sough (pronounced 'suff'), the longest of over 200 lead mine drainage soughs built throughout Derbyshire during the 18th and 19th Centuries to drain water from the labyrinth of levels and shafts far below ground. Hillcarr Sough ran underground for over four miles from Bradford Dale to drain into the River Derwent at Darley Dale. The passageway into the sough was blocked off and the river followed its original course once again.

Such a plentiful supply of fast-flowing water makes Alport an ideal spot for a watermill, indeed there has been a mill here since at least the 12th Century although the present mill buildings beside the weir in the heart of the village date from the 18th Century. Its name is derived from the Portway which crossed the river near this old mill, a prehistoric track-way that stretched north to south through the heart of the Peak District connecting settlements and religious sites including Mam Tor and Robin Hood's Stride. Despite its quiet and attractive appearance, Alport was a busy industrial village 200 years ago when it lay at the heart of the thriving lead mining industry; stories are told of the local smelt mills sending noxious fumes into the atmosphere making Alport a rather unhealthy place to live!

LATHKILL DALE is one of the five dales that make up the Derbyshire Dales National Nature Reserve and is undoubtedly the jewel in its crown. It is a world of crystal-clear streams, ancient woodland, towering crags, wild flowers and birds. From Alport, a footpath follows the River Lathkill upstream across meadows to reach Conksbury Bridge which marks the beginning (or end) of Lathkill Dale proper. There has been a bridge across the Lathkill here since at least medieval times, indeed, just to the west of the river are the earthworks and ditches of the deserted medieval village of Conksbury. There are hundreds of deserted medieval villages in this country, the result of a variety of factors including climate change, disease or a greedy landlord who saw more profit in grazing sheep for their valuable wool coats than a village full of people. Beyond Conksbury Bridge, the valley is gentle and serene with a series of low weirs built to provide good trout fishing where the clear waters tumble and cascade to create a beautiful scene framed by steep wooded slopes. The River Lathkill is said to be the purest in England and unique in that its catchment and course lie solely on limestone. *"Of all the Peakland rivers the Lathkill is the purest; its waters have the clearness and lustre of rock crystal. A lordly pleasure for a lazy man is to rest beside the pools and to watch the stealthy glidings of the great trout between the waving weeds."* **(R. Murray Gilchrist, 'The Peak District', 1911).**

But the true glory of Lathkill Dale lies beyond Lathkill Lodge where the valley gradually becomes wilder and more dramatic. The stretch of valley between Lathkill Lodge and the old mill pond of Carter's mill above Palmerston Wood (whose foundations and mill-stones are still visible) forms part of the National Nature Reserve with only a permissive path threading along the narrow valley floor; note the old sign: *"This footpath is open to visitors except Thursday in Easter week. Toll on that day one penny per person."* This path leads up through a truly wonderful landscape with the River Lathkill hemmed in by steep slopes cloaked in deciduous woodland, whilst all around is the sound of birdsong and the sweet smell of wild flowers. To the south of the river lies Meadow Place Wood, a relic of the ancient ash woodland that would have once covered the entire valley following the last Ice Age. Clearance of this woodland began as far back as Neolithic times to create pockets of grazing land and this small-scale farming continued through the centuries, indeed the name of the valley originates from the Viking words of Hlatha-ghyll that mean 'barn in a narrow valley'. However, it was during medieval times that Lathkill Dale was intensively farmed when monastic sheep flocks grazed the steep valley sides and surrounding limestone plateau, thus helping to create the flower-rich pastures of the upper valley that are still a feature today. Lead has also been mined in Lathkill Dale since at least the 13th Century, although the lead mining heyday was during the 18th and 19th Centuries. Old workings and mine levels abound including the former Mandale Mine.

This mining company was formed in 1797 but faced many obstacles from the outset. The rich veins of lead ore lay below the water table and so a drainage sough was dug through the hard limestone to drain the mines, taking a back-breaking 23 years to complete. A rich vein was eventually found, but they had to keep digging deeper to find more. In 1839 a large waterwheel was installed to drain water from deep below the drainage sough. It was fed by water from a pond at the western end of Palmerston Wood further up the valley via an artificial channel that crossed the valley over an aqueduct, the supports of which still exist. Still chasing the next rich vein, a Cornish beam engine was installed in 1847 at great expense, however, only a few years later the company ceased trading with huge debts. It is a fascinating place to explore to see the remains of the engine house, mine levels, water leat, and aqueduct. Beyond these old workings lie the remains of the Lathkill Dale Mine, established in 1825 by Thomas Bateman and John Alsop to tap into the deepest and richest part of the vein. They had to overcome flooding problems as the adjacent river flows over pervious limestone. They employed James Bateman as company agent who managed an ambitious scheme to dig a deep drainage shaft from where water was pumped out by a large 120-horsepower engine that was shielded by a house (now known as Bateman's House) where he and his family also lived. As the mines went deeper, more pumps were needed to keep the shafts dry but they could not keep the waters back and so the mine closed in 1842; in it heyday 120 miners were employed here. Steps lead down into this shaft from where you can see the main drainage shaft far below. *"Then we enter a more open part of the dale, where the rounded hillocks of brown earthy refuse and glistening spar which border the wayside, and the spades and mattocks and other mining tools and implements scatted about, indicate the metalliferous nature of the strata, and attest the character of the operations here pursued."* **(James Croston, 'On Foot through The Peak', 1889).**

Above Palmerston Wood, the character of the valley changes with sparse ash woodland, dramatic scree slopes, towering crags and a tumbling stream. Note the small waterfall of Lathkill Falls where the river flows over a tufa dam, formed as the limestone rock very slowly dissolves into the river which then leaves calcium carbonate deposits on the mosses to form a delicate honey-combed rock. Beyond the side-valley of Cales Dale, the valley grows wilder and narrower with impressive limestone outcrops looming high above - these outcrops are actually fossilised coral reefs! The path soon reaches the impressive opening of Lathkill Head Cave, the winter source of the river - only experts should enter this dangerous cave. Across to your right is a classic example of a dry limestone valley and 'fossilised' waterfall formed by meltwaters following the last Ice Age. The towering limestone outcrop that juts out between this dry limestone side-valley and the upper reaches of Lathkill Dale is known as Parson's Tor. It is named after Robert Lomas, vicar of Monyash, who fell to his death from this crag one stormy evening in 1776 on his way back from Bakewell. Upper Lathkill Dale is renowned for its springtime swathes of wild flowers, as the steep limestone grassland provides the perfect habitat for orchids, cowslips and the very rare Jacob's ladder. The head of the valley is marked by a narrow cleft in the rocks, above which is Ricklow Quarry. This old quarry once produced 'grey marble', a highly polished limestone rich in fossil crinoids that was used for fireplaces, staircases and other decorative items popular during the 18th and 19th Centuries.

Monyash

MONYASH lies sheltered amongst a fold in the rolling hills of the White Peak plateau at the head of Lathkill Dale. The name of the village either means simply 'many ash trees' or possibly 'many waters' from the Celtic word 'manais'. As with many White Peak villages, it developed around a reliable source of water as the limestone plateau is notoriously deplete of streams. A score of natural springs rose here that at one time fed four meres (clay-lined ponds), although only Fere Mere remains, which gives credence to the Celtic origins of the place-name. Monyash was recorded in the Domesday Book, indeed, the settlement pattern of today with houses grouped around the village green and strips of arable land leading back from the houses dates from the early medieval period. Beyond these narrow field strips were communal commons which were open and free from boundaries. During the Enclosure Acts of the 18th Century, these open commons were enclosed with new boundary walls built following arrow-straight lines that were planned out on maps, however, the ancient narrow strip fields around the village were also enclosed thus 'fossilising' the medieval field layout. These fields can be seen to good advantage from the path towards Magpie Mine.

Its prosperity lies firmly rooted in the local lead mining industry for this village was once a major centre where Barmote Courts were held to administer the lead mines and settle disputes. The overgrown remains of small-scale lead mining activity can be seen scattered across the surrounding countryside including bell-pits and rakes that date back to medieval times. The heyday of the industry was during the 17th to 19th Centuries when technological advances meant deeper mines and better smelting processes. Monyash was a thriving trading centre supporting this local industry with a weekly Tuesday market, annual fair and half a dozen inns. The Bull's Head remains, overlooking the attractive village green with its market cross that dates back to 1340. Next to the pub is the Old Smithy, a licensed café that welcomes walkers.

St Leonard's Church reflects the former importance of Monyash for it was founded in Norman times when the nave and chancel were built but extended and improved during the 14th Century with the addition of transepts, a wider nave, tower and imposing spire as befitting a newly established market town. It was 'restored' during the 1880s when rebuilding work took place, although much 14th Century stonework remains. Inside, there are several notable features including a fine example of a sedilia and piscine in the chancel that date back to the 12th Century, as well as a 14th Century iron-bound chest that provided secure storage for the priest's vestments, books and alter plate. During the 18th Century Monyash was also a stronghold of the Quaker movement, inspired by John Gratton, a famed Quaker preacher and writer who spread the word of the Society of Friends throughout the country. He lived in the village for 40 years during the latter half of the 17th Century.

MAGPIE MINE is one of the best preserved 19th Century lead mines in England with a fascinating range of buildings that stand gaunt against the skyline high on the limestone plateau. The White Peak plateau is a rolling landscape of fields peppered with dew ponds, woodland copse, farmsteads and cosy villages. But these agricultural fields belie an industrial history that stretches back 2,000 years with old bell pits and overgrown workings scattered across the landscape. Lead ore has been mined in the Peak District since at least Roman times with small-scale production taking place right through to the Middle Ages. Its heyday was during the 17th to 19th Centuries when drainage soughs coupled with new technology meant that the mines could go deeper in search of lead ore and the Peak District became one of the richest and most productive lead mining areas in the world. Dwindling reserves and cheaper imports during the late 19th Century heralded the demise of the industry with the last big mine closing in 1939.

Lead mining began here in the 1740s when there were several small-scale mining companies working the different (or sometimes the same) veins. These competing companies often came to blows. In 1833 three miners were killed when the Magpie miners, working the North Bole vein, broke through to the Great Redsoil vein that was being worked by the neighbouring Maypitt miners. An acrimonious dispute ensued that was brought before the Barmote Court, however, the miners took it upon themselves to light fires of straw and tar within the mines to 'smoke out' the other miners but sadly three Maypitt miners were killed by the fumes. The miners were brought to court but acquitted because, it was said, blame lay on both sides and the Magpie miners were defending their mine. In revenge, the distraught widows put a curse of the Magpie Mine and the company went bankrupt just two years later; the Widow's Curse remains to this day. The mine is also reputedly haunted by the ghosts of these murdered miners.

The Magpie Mine re-opened in 1839 working both the North Bole and Great Redsoil veins and a year later a Cornish beam engine was installed to pump water from the mines. Flooding was still a problem and so work began on the Magpie Sough, a drainage tunnel that runs for 2 km up to a depth of 175 metres below ground to drain into the River Wye near Ashford in the Water. This tunnel took 8 years to complete and was finished in 1881 at great expense. The beam engine now only had to drain water from below the level of Magpie Sough but the mine still had mixed fortunes, especially during the first few decades of the 20th Century when it closed several times. Following the Second World War, there was an ambitious plan to re-open the mine but little lead was found and it finally closed in 1954.

The ruins of Magpie Mine are a fascinating yet rather eerie place to explore with old buildings, spoil heaps and chimneys all around as well as a 222-metre deep shaft surmounted by winding gear and a cage that dates from the 1950s. The bottom 47-metres of the shaft are flooded, above which level the water is drained by way of the Magpie Sough. The large stone-built Cornish Engine House and adjacent round Cornish chimney are particularly impressive, whilst nearby is a circular gunpowder store, the mine agent's house, smithy and a replica horse-gin. These extensive and evocative remains offer a unique insight into the once flourishing lead mining industry and stand in silent tribute to the many thousands of men who toiled underground in appalling conditions in search of lead ore. The site is cared for by the Peak District Mines Historical Society.

SHELDON is a quiet village situated on a sloping shelf of land high on the White Peak plateau above the wooded banks of the deeply incised Wye Valley. Mainly 18th Century cottages and farms line the single street, set back behind a long and narrow green that runs almost the entire length of the village. In the heart of the village stands quite an unusual pub for it is hard to believe that the welcoming Cock & Pullet was a derelict barn just over ten years ago. Great attention to detail has created a wonderfully cosy bar that belies its true age for you feel as though you are sitting in a time-mellowed country inn that has been here for centuries. This relatively new pub stands next to the former Devonshire Arms that has been closed for many years. An old ash tree once grew on the green in front of this former pub. Back in 1601, a duck was seen to fly into this tree and disappear then, when they cut the tree down some 300 years later and the trunk was cut into planks, there was an imprint in the shape of a duck! Up until the mid 19th Century a small chapel-of-ease stood on one of these central greens, first recorded in the 15th Century and dedicated to All Saints. The small Parish Church of St Michael and All Angels lies along a track just off the main street, built in 1865 using stones recovered from the old chapel. This church is noted for its large and steeply pitched roof.

DEEP DALE is one of many side-valleys that feed the River Wye. Our route follows a steep path down through woodland to reach the bottom of this valley, much of which is protected as a Nature Reserve as well as a Site of Special Scientific Interest. The valley is renowned for its spring display of wild flowers when over a million cowslips carpet the steep grassy valley sides along with great swathes of early-purple orchids and many other flowers and plants including meadow saxifrage, mountain pansy and columbine. The valley is also steeped in legend for the dark and uninviting gully at the mouth of the valley is known as Dimin Dale, or Demon's Dell, where demons are supposed to live - you have been warned!

THE RIVER WYE rises on the wild moors of Axe Edge just to the south of Buxton, from where the infant river flows eastwards through Buxton along artificial channels before skirting huge quarries. The character of the valley then changes dramatically as it cuts a deep swathe through the White Peak plateau. Its aesthetic qualities constantly but subtly change as the river valley meanders from west to east through the heart of the Peak District, reflected by its numerous name changes including Chee Dale, Miller's Dale, Water-cum-Jolly Dale and finally Monsal Dale, which is where we join this delightful valley. This is a landscape of gleaming limestone scars, deep wooded valleys, abundant wildlife and glorious views. At Ashford in the Water, the River Wye leaves the limestone gorge behind and meanders through a broader valley of rich pastures and woodland copse to soon swell the River Derwent at Rowsley. The walk up through this valley from White Lodge to Monsal Head is an absolute delight as you follow the sparsely wooded riverside pastures as the valley gracefully curves round beneath towering slopes that are crowned by Fin Cop, an Iron Age hill-fort. The path passes a dramatic weir and then slants up through woodland to reach Monsal Head and the celebrated view across the valley with the famous viaduct dominating, its huge arches rising 80-ft above the river.

THE MONSAL TRAIL is an eight-and-a-half mile walking route between Bakewell and Chee Dale along the cinder track-bed of the former Midland Railway route from London to Manchester. From Derby, the railway followed the Derwent Valley as far as Rowsley before heading west up through the limestone valleys of the River Wye to Buxton. The railway reached Rowsley in 1849, Buxton in 1863 and finally Manchester in 1867, the construction of which was extremely controversial particularly the section through Monsal Dale and Miller's Dale, which caused a national outcry with John Ruskin lamenting...

"There was a rocky valley between Buxton and Bakewell, once upon a time as divine as the Vale of Tempe; you might have seen the Gods there morning and evening – Apollo and all the sweet Muses of the light – walking in fair procession on the lawns of it, and to and fro among the pinnacles of its crags. You cared neither for Gods or cash (which you did not know the way to get) you thought you could get it by what the Times calls 'Railway Enterprise'. You enterprised a railroad through the valley – you blasted its rocks away, heaped thousands of tons of shale into its lovely stream. The valley is gone and the Gods with it, and now every fool in Buxton can be at Bakewell in half and hour and every fool in Bakewell at Buxton; which you think a lucrative process of exchange – you fools everywhere."

For over a century this railway flourished and was renowned as one of the most scenic in England with a series of dark tunnels and then incredible views as the trains sped along the line up through the narrow limestone gorge. There was a large station at Miller's Dale further up the valley at the junction of the main line to Manchester and the branch line to Buxton, as well as a smaller station at Upperdale in Monsal Dale itself. Imagine the scene with express trains bound for London, goods trains loaded with quicklime from the quarries and local trains full of tourists heading to the spa town of Buxton. *"At times a hollow rumble sounds in the far distance, increases and increases, and the lighted train flies across the viaduct, and, passing the little station, disappears in the farther tunnel. But for this connection with modern life Monsal Dale would belong altogether to the distant past."* **(R. Murray Gilchrist, 1911).** The railway between Matlock and Buxton succumbed to Beeching's axe in 1968 and was disused for 12 years before being taken over by the Peak District National Park, who then created the Monsal Trail walking route. Time is a great healer and the embankments and viaducts have become a much loved part of the landscape as well as a haven for wildlife. Our route follows this old track-bed across the famous Monsal Viaduct before passing Monsal Dale Station to reach the blocked-up Cressbrook Tunnel - it's full steam ahead along this section of the walk!

Cressbrook Mill

CRESSBROOK MILL was first established in 1783 by Richard Arkwright, the 'Father of the Factory System', although the original cotton mill burnt down just two years after it had been built and was replaced by what is known as the Old Mill. In 1815, a much larger mill (the 'Big Mill') was built by Arkwright's agent William Newton, mill manager and self-educated poet who became known as the 'Minstrel of the Peak'. This magnificent Georgian building is capped by a small bell-cote that once summoned the workers, mostly child apprentices brought from city workhouses or orphanages to work. Unlike neighbouring Litton Mill, Newton was said to have treated his child workforce relatively well with decent accommodation in a row of cottages behind the mill known as Apprentices Row as well as edible food, schooling and even some time off, although some contemporary accounts challenge this view. Above the mill complex perched high on the hillside is the village of Cressbrook, which developed during the 1830s when Cressbrook Mill was under the ownership of McConnel & Company. It was built as a model village with rows of cottages, a school and the grand Cressbrook Hall, home of the mill owner. The mill closed in 1965 and has recently been converted into apartments.

WATER-CUM-JOLLY DALE is a valley of still waters, gleaming limestone cliffs and thickly wooded riverbanks that are teeming with wildlife. The waters of the River Wye are held back behind a weir that has created a small lake that floods much of the valley, built originally to create a head of water to power the waterwheels of Cressbrook Mill. The initial part of the walk up through Water-cum-Jolly Dale follows a delightful path that is squeezed between limestone bluffs and the mill pond with water lapping across the path in places. The river is broad and still, choked with reeds, decaying trees and marsh grass. Water voles plop into the water, dippers bow on branches and trout rise from the river to catch a fly. The valley twists and turns beneath towering cliffs cloaked with ancient ash woodland. The valley changes its name to Miller's Dale as it curves round to reach the old mill complex at Litton Mill, although the village of Miller's Dale lies just over a mile further upstream. The path through Water-cum-Jolly Dale to Litton Mill is concessionary, so please tread carefully! *"From Cressbrook to Litton Mill, a distance of more than a mile, the margin of the stream is but rarely traversed by human foot. It is only after a long dry season that this can be accomplished, and then the effort is attended with considerable risk and danger – a narrow shelving ledge of rock, on which the hand of art has never ventured to exercise itself, being the only footing afforded."* (**James Croston, 1889**).

LITTON MILL dates back to 1782 and was built in this remote valley to be close to water power but far away from the Luddites of the towns. During the early 19th Century, this old cotton mill became notorious for the cruel treatment of its child workforce by mill owner Ellis Needham, which only came to light after one of the former child apprentices called Robert Blincoe went public with his story. Robert Blincoe was sent to the St Pancras Workhouse in London when he was only four years old and by the age of six he was working as a chimney sweep. In 1802 when he was eleven he was sent to work at Litton Mill virtually as a child slave where he stayed for several years until he left the mill at the end of his apprenticeship in 1814. He then moved to Manchester where, through hard work and good fortune, he successfully built up his own cotton company. Years later, Blincoe told his story to a local journalist called John Brown, an advocate of factory reform, who was so fascinated by Blincoe's account of his life as a child apprentice that he penned his biography and called it 'A Memoir of Robert Blincoe, an Orphan Boy.' In 1828 this harrowing account of life at Litton Mill was published as a series of newspaper articles, an event that shocked the nation. Blincoe's story detailed how poor and orphaned children were brought to this mill as cheap labour from London and were made to work long hours in terrible conditions with meagre food. Many children died of disease or ill treatment and were buried in unmarked graves in Tideswell churchyard. Charles Dickens is said to have based Oliver Twist on Blincoe. The mill closed in the 1960s and has recently been converted into apartments, but a sense of sadness prevails.

TIDESWELL DALE, the seventh and last limestone dale along today's walk, is a large side-valley that strikes northwards from the River Wye in sinuous curves up to reach Tideswell that lies sheltered in its upper reaches. Most of Tideswell Dale is owned by the National Park Authority who have transformed an old basalt quarry into a delightful nature reserve with riverside paths, woodland walks and a sculpture trail. Basalt is an extremely hard igneous rock that flowed as lava across the limestone many millions of years ago to create a band of hard rock known locally as 'toadstone'.

TIDESWELL, known locally as 'Tidsa', is a place of great charm with numerous lanes and small squares beckoning you to explore. It feels more like a town than a village, mainly because it was once an important trading centre with a market charter dating back to 1251 and also where the Great Courts of the Royal Forest of the Peak once convened. The weekly markets are no more but the Market Square can be found at the top of the High Street whilst the smaller Pot Market lies adjacent to the church. Some say its name is derived from the famous Ebbing and Flowing Well, one of the original 'Seven Wonders of the Peak' as described by Thomas Hobbes in 1636 in what was the first guide to the region. The other 'Wonders' were Peak Cavern, Poole's Cavern, Eldon Hole, St Ann's Well, Mam Tor and Chatsworth House. However, this Ebbing and Flowing Well is actually a few miles away in Barmoor Clough, although a dried-up spring in a garden along Manchester Road also claims the title. In reality, Tideswell takes its name from a Saxon farmer called Tidi. It remained a small farming community until the Norman Conquest when this area was given to William Peverel, who built his castle overlooking present-day Castleton. In the Middle Ages Tideswell developed as a market centre for the southern part of the Royal Forest of the Peak, the vast hunting preserve administered from Peveril Castle, and it also prospered from lead mining and wool.

This wealth is reflected in the magnificent Church of St John the Baptist - the 'Cathedral of the Peak'. Built between 1350 and 1399 on the site of a smaller Norman church, it is the most complete medieval church in the Peak District and a superb example of late Decorated Gothic and early Perpendicular architecture. The building was financed by the Foljambe and Meverell families, both of which were prominent, wealthy and well connected. Inside, the spacious nave and chancel are awash with wonderful carvings, brasses and memorials; of particular note are the intricately carved chancel screen and choir stalls as well as exquisite oak carvings by local craftsman Advent Hunstone. *"Another notable point is the recent oak carving, the work of a self-taught local artist whose skill has been called into play as visitors' contributions go on helping to beautify this finest church of a district richer in subterranean fanes fit for diabolic rites than in ecclesiastic architecture."* **(A. R. Hope Moncrieff, 'The**

Peak Country', 1908). Look out for the brass memorial to Bishop Robert Pursglove, who was born at Tideswell in 1504. He founded Tideswell Grammar School in 1560 and was Prior of Guisborough at the time of its dissolution when he was pensioned off and later became Bishop of Hull before returning to Tideswell to retire where he died in 1579. Interestingly, he served as a prior under Henry VIII and bishop under the Protestant Edward VI as well as Catholic Mary Tudor but refused to change allegiance a fourth time and swear the oath of Supremacy under Elizabeth I, which led to the loss of his bishopric. The former Grammar School still overlook the churchyard on its north side, although the present buildings date from the 18th Century and are now used as the library. Also of note is the 15th Century alabaster tomb of Sir Sampson Meverell, Knight Constable of England who fought in eleven wars against France who lies in a tomb in the chancel whilst nearby is the 15th Century tomb of John Foljambe. In the churchyard lies Samuel Slack who died in 1822, a singer who rose from obscurity to national renown touring the country and even performing for George III *"...that noble, deep-toned melodist..."*. He famously scared off a bull with the roar of his voice! William Newton, the 'Minstrel of the Peak', also lies buried in the churchyard.

Tideswell

STAGE FIVE

TIDESWELL
to
CASTLETON

✦

"I walked through Eyam taking note of the many interpretative signs that adorned nearly every wall, but it was a simple solitary grave in a field just above the village that made me stop and think. What pain and terror must those poor souls have endured during the terrible months the Plague cast its dark shadow over the village. This sad and lonely grave spoke more of their anguish than anything else. They would have looked across this field, as I was doing now, with hearts full of sadness and minds full of fear. The past and present came very close as I stood there looking back to the village where desperate families once dragged the dead from their homes to lay them to rest in a field. Their torment was still tangible."

Mark Reid
July 2006

WALK INFORMATION

Points of interest:	Derbyshire's last gibbet, a silly dale and a foolish village, a tale of self sacrifice, the finest Saxon preaching cross in Derbyshire, wonderful views from wild moorland, a hidden wooded clough, walking in the footsteps of Romans and the church of the foresters.

Distance:

Tideswell to Eyam	6 miles
Eyam to Castleton	8 miles
Total	14 miles

Time: Allow 6 - 7 hours

Terrain: A quiet road leads from Tideswell to Litton from where a grassy/stony path drops down into Cressbrook Dale. A grassy path heads up along the valley floor (wet conditions after rain) to reach the A623 at Wardlow Mires from where field paths lead across the White Peak plateau over a succession of wall-stiles to Foolow then on across more fields to Eyam. A lane then a path climbs steeply up onto Eyam Edge to join the walled track of Sir William Hill Road. A narrow path then heads across Eyam Moor with a fairly steep descent to reach an escarpment above Bretton Clough (steep drops to side of path) from where a grassy track leads steadily down into the wooded confines of Bretton Clough. A broad path then steadily climbs up through wooded Abney Clough to reach Abney from where a narrow lane rises up to join a junction of tracks on Abney Moor. A stony track skirts around Over Dale then drops steadily down to reach

Brough. Clear field and riverside paths lead through the Hope Valley to Castleton.
Expect muddy or flooded conditions after rain in all of the valleys. Limestone is slippery when wet. Take care crossing the A623 at Wardlow Mires and B6049 at Brough.

Ascents:	Eyam Moor: 407 metres
	Brough Lane (Abney Moor): 380 metres
Viewpoints:	Views throughout Cressbrook Dale.
	Eyam Edge looking across the White Peak.
	Eyam Moor looking northwards towards Win Hill and the Eastern Edges.
	Bretton Clough from Eyam Moor.
	Views across the Hope Valley from Brough Lane.

FACILITIES

· ·

Tideswell	Inn / B&B / Shop / PO / Café / Bus / Phone / Toilets / YH
Litton	Inn / B&B / Shop / PO / Bus / Phone
Wardlow Mires	Inn / Café / Bus / Phone
Foolow	Inn / B&B / Bus / Phone
Eyam	Inn / B&B / Shop / PO / Café / Bus / Phone / Toilets / YH
Abney	Phone / Camp
Brough	Inn / Bus
Hope	Inn / B&B / Shop / PO / Café / Bus / Train / Phone / Toilets / Camp
Castleton	Inn / B&B / Shop / PO / Café / Bus / Phone / Toilets / Info / YH / Camp

ROUTE DESCRIPTION

(Map Thirteen)

From the small square in front of the main gates to Tideswell Church (with your back to the church) turn right along Commercial Road passing the NatWest Bank and follow this road down through the village passing the Horse & Jockey pub to reach the last of the houses at the bottom edge of Tideswell where you take the narrow lane branching up to the left (The Lodge). This lane soon levels out by some cottages (Tideswell Dale and B6049 down to your right) where you carry straight on along the lane for approx. 0.25 miles then follow it bending sharp left down to join the road through Litton Dale (limestone side-valley). Turn left along this road (pavement on right-hand side) and follow this up into Litton. Follow the main road curving round to the right across the village green towards 'Wardlow, Cressbrook' (ignore turning towards 'Cressbrook, Monsal Dale) then, as reach the end of the village green (100 yards after the Cressbrook turning), turn right along a track immediately before Litton View (house) then left after a few paces over a wall-stile immediately after the house (do not enter the farmyard). After the wall-stile head diagonally across the middle of the field to reach a wall-stile in the far left corner that leads onto a walled track. Turn left along the track for 25 yards then right over a wall-stile beside a gate (SP), after which head straight on across the middle of the field to join the wall on your left then, where this wall bends sharply away, head to the left down across the field to reach a wall-stile tucked away beside a small 'dog leg' in the wall half-way down the hillside. Cross the stile and follow the path to the right down into Tansley Dale (grassy side-valley). Follow the clear path to the left heading along the floor of this dry limestone valley all the way down until it emerges out into Cressbrook Dale where you reach a small gate in a wall along the floor of the valley. Head through the wall-gate and over some stepping stones just beyond (stream often dry), after which turn left and follow the grassy path heading up along the valley floor alongside the wall on your left. After just under 0.5 miles, the path follows the valley as it sweeps round to the right then passes below the conspicuous outcrop of Peter's Stone (path climbs up slightly as it passes below this outcrop). After Peter's Stone, carry straight on up through the valley (still with the wall on your left) for just over 0.25 miles then, as you approach the head of the valley, the broad grassy path becomes enclosed by walls on either side that gradually close in to 'funnel' you to a gate at the head of the valley that leads into the yard of Brookside Farm. Bear left through the farmyard to reach the A623 beside its junction with the B6465 *(take care - fast road)*.

Cross the A623 and turn right along this main road passing the Three Stags Heads, just after which turn left along a track into a farmyard (SP) where you head to the left along a track passing between the barns (stone-built barn on your left) then, where this track bends sharp right at the end of this stone barn, bear off to the right along the edge of the farmyard to quickly reach a small metal gate tucked away behind a low barn that leads out onto a field. Head straight on alongside the wall on your left up across two fields (heading towards Stanley House Farm ahead) then bear slightly left up across the third field to reach a wall-stile beside a gate in the top left corner just to the left of Stanley House Farm that leads onto a lane beside the farm entrance. Turn right along the lane passing the farm buildings on your right (lane becomes a stony track) and continue along this walled track then, where it bends sharp left as you reach the foot of Silly Dale, turn right (off this bend) along a walled grassy path. Follow this walled path for 25 yards down into the bottom of the shallow valley then cross the wall-stile to the left (SP), immediately after which turn right up through a wall-gap. After the wall-gap, head straight on bearing very slightly left up across two fields to re-join the walled grassy path (SP). Cross the wall-stile opposite (SP) and follow the clear path straight on gradually bearing to the left up across several fields over a succession of wall-stiles for almost 0.5 miles to reach a kissing gate set in a field corner on the edge of Foolow. Head through the kissing gate then turn right across the narrow field to reach a gate in the left-hand field corner just after a house that leads onto an enclosed narrow path which you follow to emerge onto the village green in the centre of Foolow.

Walk across the village green passing the pond and stone cross on your left then follow the road straight on passing the Bull's Head and follow it straight on out of the village towards 'Eyam, Grindleford'. Continue along the road for about 250 yards then, immediately after the Foolow village sign, take the FP to the right over a wall-stile (SP). Bear left across the field and through a small wall-gate that leads onto the end of a rough walled track beside a ruinous barn (SP 'Eyam'). Head straight over the track and follow the path alongside the wall on your right over a series of wall-stiles and down into the shallow valley of Linen Dale. Head through the squeeze-stile/wall-gate at the bottom of the valley (SP 'Eyam'), then bear slightly left up the grassy bank, over a tumbledown wall and on across the next field to reach a wall-gate (SP). After this wall-gate, head straight on across the field and through another wall-gate, after which carry straight on across the next field over a tumbledown wall across your path then continue on alongside a wall on your right to reach a wall-gate beside a gate in the field corner that leads onto a walled track. At the track, head through the squeeze-stile opposite and follow the path across several fields over a further five stiles (Eyam comes into view after the fifth stile). Continue straight on gradually dropping down the hillside alongside the wall on your right and through a squeeze-stile in the bottom right corner of the field, after which follow the path straight on across three more fields then along a narrow path between some houses to join Tideswell Lane on the outskirts of Eyam. Cross the lane and follow the FP opposite (SP) straight on across the field to quickly join another lane, where you take the enclosed FP opposite to the right. Follow this down to emerge in a small housing development where you head straight on down to join the main road through Eyam (Church Street). Turn right along this road and follow it through the village passing Eyam Hall then St Lawrence's Church on to reach The Square in the centre of Eyam.

As you reach The Square, turn left along Water Lane passing the Miners' Arms on your right and follow this lane rising steadily up out of the village passing some water troughs on your right, after which the lane climbs steeply up to reach a bench at the top of the lane after the last house on your right. At the top of the lane, take the FP to the left through a small gate (SP), after which follow the path gradually bearing to the right up across the hillside to reach a gate in the top far field corner that leads onto a road. At the road, take the FP opposite to the left (SP) and follow the path (steps) slanting up to the left across the steep wooded hillside to reach a wall at the end of the steps (above Eyam Youth Hostel hidden amongst trees), where you carry straight on climbing steeply up alongside the wall on your left. Where this wall bends round to the left and levels out at the top of the woods, follow the path slanting up across the steep grassy bank to reach a small wall-gate in the top left field corner at the top of the steep bank (Eyam Edge). Head through this wall-gate and walk straight on keeping close to the top of the wooded bank on your left and through another wall-gate in the field corner, after which bear right up across two fields to join a road.

Turn left along the road for a few paces then right over a wall-stile (SP). After the wall-stile, head straight on up across the field alongside the wall on your right. After a while the field levels out (transmitter mast to your left) - continue straight on alongside the wall to reach a wall-stile in the field corner that leads onto the enclosed track of Sir William Hill Road. Cross the wall-stile opposite (SP 'Stoke Ford') and follow the path straight on across Eyam Moor for 0.25 miles to reach the brow of a steep bank beside a stone cairn *(superb views)*. Continue straight on along the clear path down the steep bank then gradually drop down across the moorland along a grassy/rocky path to reach a gate set in a narrow corner of the boundary wall at the bottom of Eyam Moor. Cross the stile beside the left-hand gate, after which follow the wide grassy path straight on alongside the wall on your right gently dropping down (steep escarpment to your left above Bretton Clough), passing some gritstone outcrops where the path curves round to the right (wall still on your right) down to reach another stile beside a gate. Cross the stile and continue along the wide grassy path gently dropping down then, after a while, the path gradually bears to the left away from the wall heading more steeply down across the hillside to reach the top of a steep wooded bank. Follow the path to the left across the top of this wooded bank then winding down to join a clear path just above Bretton Brook, where you turn right down to quickly reach a junction of paths and a FB across Bretton Brook at Stoke Ford.

Cross the FB and over a stile just beyond, after which turn right over another FB across Abney Brook just after which turn left (SP 'Abney') along a clear path that leads into woodland. Follow the wide path heading straight on through wooded Abney Clough, with the stream just down to your left, steadily climbing up for almost 0.5 miles to reach a bridlegate across the path. Head through the gate and carry straight on up through the valley - the path soon narrows and becomes rougher underfoot and leads up through woodland/undergrowth to reach two old stone gateposts and a wall. Pass through these old gateposts and follow the narrow path straight on, with a fence/field boundary on your right, heading up through the valley walking through woodland/undergrowth. After a while the path emerges from the woodland - carry straight on along the narrow path across rough pastures then, as you approach the head of the valley where it opens out slightly (telegraph poles criss-cross the valley), follow the fence/field boundary on your right bending up to quickly reach a gate that leads onto a rough enclosed track which you follow up to reach the road through Abney.

Turn left along the road and follow it gently rising up through Abney then, as you reach the village hall and 'phone box, turn right along a narrow lane. Follow this lane steadily rising up for just over 0.5 miles to reach a gate at the top (and end) of the metalled lane, just beyond which you reach a crossroads of stony tracks. Turn left (SP 'Brough') along the stony track alongside wall on your left (and tumbledown wall on your right) and follow this track curving round to the right around the head of Over Dale (Abney Moor to your left) to reach a gateway across the track after 0.5 miles. Head through the gateway and carry straight on along the enclosed stony track for a further 1.25 miles heading across the top of a broad ridge of land (keep to the stony track all the way) then gradually dropping down, with Over Dale falling steeply away to your right and views ahead across the Hope Valley, to eventually join a metalled lane at the entrance to Elmore Hill Farm. Carry straight on down along the lane then bending sharply down to the left to reach the B6049 at Brough *(Travellers Rest 250 yard detour to right)*.

Turn left along the road and over a bridge across Bradwell Brook after a short distance, immediately after which turn right through a gate (SP 'Hope & Castleton via the Roman Station Anavio'). Head straight up across the field to reach a ladder stile over a fence beside a gateway on the edge of the Roman fort (information plaque). Walk straight across the middle of the fort (grassy earthworks), which you quickly cross, then carry straight on to quickly reach a small FB across a wooded stream. After the FB, head alongside the fence/woodland on your left and follow this curving round to the left then straight on along the top field edge to reach a stile beside a gate, after which carry straight on alongside the fence/woodland on your left heading up across the fairly narrow field then, about three-quarters of the way across this field, head right down along a sunken track and through squeeze-stile beside a gate in a section of wall. After this gate, follow the grassy track straight on gently dropping down across the middle of the field then, as you reach the end of the field, head along a short section of enclosed track to join a road through a gate. Turn right down along the road to reach a T-junction on the edge of Hope *(Hope short detour to right)*.

At this T-junction, turn left up along the road for 25 yards then take the FP to the right over a stile beside a gate (SP 'Castleton'). After the stile, follow the narrow path to the right along the field edge across the top of a wooded bank above Peakshole Water - follow this path along the top of this wooded riverbank for 0.5 miles across fields to reach the cement works railway line. Cross the railway line *(take care)* and walk straight on alongside the fence/Peakshole Water on your right at first then across the field bearing very slightly away from the fence passing to the right of a small tree-covered mound and on to reach a stile beside a small metal gate in a wall across your path. Cross this stile and head straight on across three fields over a succession of stiles, then continue straight on alongside a fence on your left to join the banks of Peakshole Water again on your right at the end of this field. Follow the fence/ riverbank bending round to the right then straight on to reach a stile beside a gate that leads onto a track. Follow this track straight on then

bending around some barns (leaving Peakshole Water behind) to reach
the main road through Castleton. Turn left into the centre of Castleton.

Foolow

MAP THIRTEEN

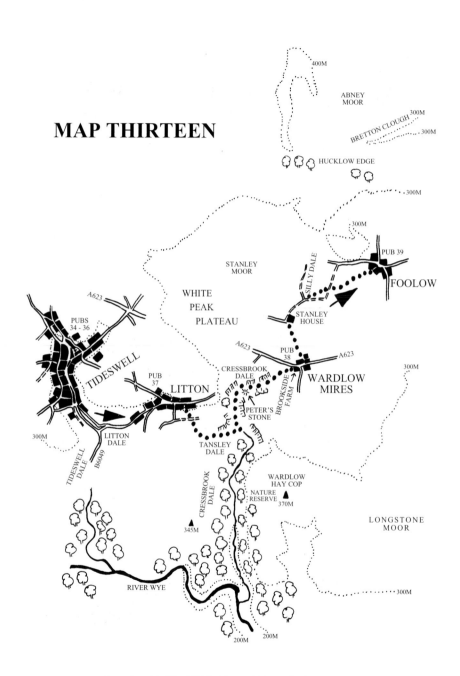

400M

ABNEY
MOOR

BRETTON CLOUGH 300M
300M

HUCKLOW EDGE

300M

300M

PUB 39

STANLEY
MOOR

SILLY DALE

FOOLOW

WHITE
PEAK
PLATEAU

A623

PUBS
34 - 36

STANLEY
HOUSE

A623

PUB
38

A623

300M

TIDESWELL

PUB
37

LITTON

CRESSBROOK
DALE

WARDLOW
MIRES

BROOKSIDE
FARM

PETER'S
STONE

300M

LITTON
DALE

TIDESWELL
DALE

B6049

TANSLEY
DALE

CRESSBROOK
DALE

WARDLOW
HAY COP

NATURE
RESERVE

370M

LONGSTONE
MOOR

345M

RIVER WYE

300M

200M

200M

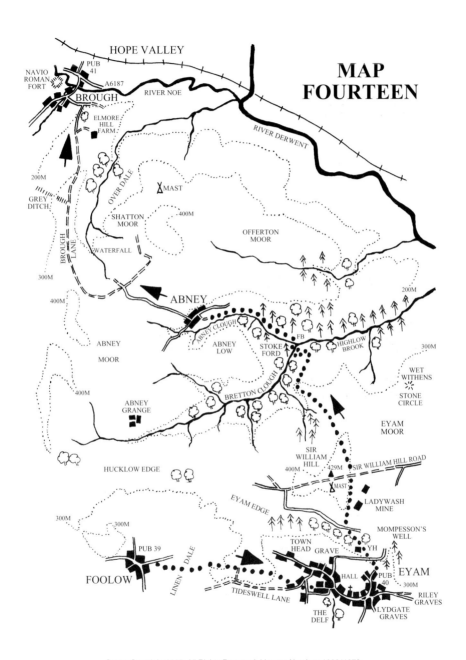

MAP
FOURTEEN

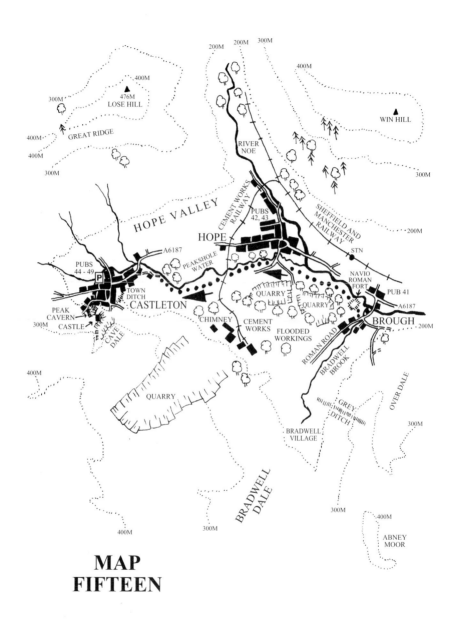

MAP
FIFTEEN

LITTON lies high on the limestone plateau on the 300-metre contour line between the upper reaches of Cressbrook Dale and Tideswell Dale, from where a small valley known as Litton Dale leads up to the village, threaded by a road. Unlike its grand namesake in the Yorkshire Dales, this valley is small, dry and not particularly impressive, but pleasant enough. Litton is a classic White Peak village with attractive 17th and 18th Century farms and cottages, many with datestones, crowding around a spacious tree-shaded green complete with ancient stepped cross and stocks overlooked by the Red Lion, one of Peakland's most authentic pubs. It was the local lead mines that brought prosperity to this village, but the mines have long since closed. Both Litton and Tideswell hold their famous well dressing ceremonies at the same time each June, amongst the finest in the Peak District.

William Bagshawe, the 'Apostle of the Peak', was born at Litton in 1628. A member of one of Derbyshire's oldest families, he was appointed Vicar of Glossop but his refusal to accept the Act of Uniformity in 1662 following the restoration of Charles II, which required ceremonies to follow the Common Book of Prayer as well as Episcopal ordination of ministers, meant that he (and 2,000 other clergymen) left his post to become a Non-Conformist preacher who travelled from village to village, despite warrants for his arrest. The Act of Toleration in 1689 allowed Non-Conformists to preach without fear of prosecution. Bagshawe lies buried in St Thomas á Becket Church at Chapel-en-le-Frith.

The drystone walls that surround the village are historically very important for they stand as some of the best examples of 'fossilised' medieval village fields in England. Many centuries ago, the village was surrounded by open village fields that consisted of narrow strips of land farmed by individual villagers, beyond which were the open communal fields and commons. During the 18th and 19th Centuries these ancient fields were enclosed by stone walls that 'fossilised' the medieval field pattern. A glance at the map reveals an amazing cobweb of tiny rectangular medieval fields around Litton beyond which are the larger fields that were planned on paper when the communal fields and commons were divided up as part of the Enclosure Acts.

CRESSBROOK DALE, a major tributary of the River Wye, is one of the five dales that make up the Derbyshire Dales National Nature Reserve. The southern half of this valley is thickly cloaked with semi-ancient ash woodland that clings to the steep valley sides. This is a world of dense trees, moss-covered walls, clear streams, wild flowers and birds where you will find the highest concentration of plant species per square metre in the whole of Derbyshire. *"An abundance of water-cress is nurtured upon the margin and in the channel of the stream, round which the water bubbles in limpid rills, then rattles merrily on over the shining pebbles, murmuring its admiration of the surrounding beauty in a thousand songs of joyousness."* **(James Croston, "On Foot through The Peak", 1889).** The northern half of the valley has a completely different character with sweeping hillsides, flower-rich grassland, limestone crags and shattered scree slopes dotted with trees. A path leads down from Litton via the delightful side-valley of Tansley Dale to emerge out into Cressbrook Dale amidst a wondrous landscape. Visit in spring and the hillsides will be awash with colour as thousands of early purple orchids and cowslips come into flower, not to mention rarer plants such as dwarf thistle and lesser meadow rue. This valley is managed by Natural England who has recently introduced six Exmoor ponies to graze the limestone grasslands during summer and autumn. These hardy animals graze coarse grasses and scrub bushes that cows and sheep would otherwise leave behind, thus reducing the need for manual cutting or burning to maintain the flower-rich grasslands, which rely on thin alkaline soils. Near the head of the valley is Peter's Stone, a huge lump of detached limestone rock that is slowly slipping down the hillside. Its domed appearance is said to resemble St Peter's Basilica in Rome. This was the site of the last gibbet in Derbyshire in 1815 when Anthony Linguard murdered the Wardlow Mires toll-bar keeper and was subsequently sentenced to death by hanging. His body was gibbeted on Peter's Stone as a warning to others.

The upper reaches of Cressbrook Dale are usually dry except after heavy rain when a stream flows down alongside the old wall that threads along the valley floor. The very head of the valley is actually quite marshy as several springs rise to the surface, providing the perfect habitat for the increasingly rare water vole. The hamlet of Wardlow Mires marks the head of Cressbrook Dale, famed for its old-fashioned and completely unspoilt pub, a classic example of how country pubs used to be. Wardlow Mires is well named indeed for it is set in a shallow hollow on the White Peak plateau surrounded by springs and boggy ground.

Cressbrook Dale

FOOLOW is arguably the Peak District's prettiest village, situated near the northern limits of the White Peak with the escarpment of Hucklow Edge and Eyam Edge just to the north, which mark the beginning of the Dark Peak. A delightful mix of old farms, houses, cottages, chapels and a fine country pub cluster around a village green complete with duck pond, enclosed well, 14th Century stepped cross and bull ring. The cross was originally a boundary marker of the Royal Forest of the Peak. The name of the village was probably derived from a Saxon farmer called 'Foo' who gave his name to a nearby hill or 'low' - and nothing to do with the local village idiot, although just to the west is a dry limestone valley called Silly Dale! The footpath between Foolow and Eyam Edge crosses the 'boundary' between the White and Dark Peak - see if you can spot where the underlying rocks change.

EYAM, pronounced 'Eem', is one of the most famous villages in England due to the altruism of its inhabitants during the 17th Century when it was gripped by an outbreak of plague. Disease was a fact of life in medieval England; what sets Eyam apart is the tale of selfless heroism. In September 1665 a box of cloth arrived from London for local tailor George Viccars who was lodging with the Hadfield family in a house near the church. The cloth was damp and so he laid it out in front of the fire to dry. Unbeknownst to him, the cloth was home to plague-infected fleas. Within days he had died, and within a few weeks several other villagers had also died. Panic spread and some people began to flee the village. Fearing the infection would spread to neighbouring villages, the local Rector William Mompesson along with the Non-Conformist preacher Thomas Stanley, asked the villagers to voluntarily quarantine themselves. Food and supplies were left at the parish boundary stones dotted on the outskirts of the village where money was left in vinegar-filled holes in return for the supplies. *"For a year they remained cut off from the world, fed by supplies which were left for them on the plague-stricken boundary; and a well is shown in which they are said to have left their money in exchange, though soon they could have no money to give, and their sustenance depended on charity organised by the Earl of Devonshire, Lord-Lieutenant of the county, who through this trying year nobly stuck to his post at Chatsworth, a few miles off."* **(A. R. Hope Moncrieff, 'The Peak Country', 1908).** The church was closed and open-air services were held in the wooded valley of Cucklet Delf just to the south of the village. Whole families were wiped out and people buried their dead in fields around their houses. At Riley Farm just outside Eyam, Mrs Hancock lost her husband and six children within the space of eight days during August 1666 and had to bury them herself in an adjacent field; surprisingly Mrs Hancock survived. Then there is the sad tale of Rowland Torre from Stoney Middleton who secretly met his sweetheart Emmott Sydall in the Delf during 1666 when they would call to each other across the rocky valley. One day, Emmott failed to turn up for their meeting but Rowland convinced himself that the villagers had stopped her from coming to see him. When the Plague finally ended, Rowland was the first person to enter Eyam in search of his sweetheart but she had died from the Plague. By the time the Plague ended in October 1666, around 260 people had died out of a village population of 350, although the two ministers were amongst the survivors. Despite the terrible loss, their efforts were successful and the disease did not spread. Information plaques around the village bring this incredibly moving tale of self-sacrifice to life; the solitary graves dotted around the fields are particularly poignant. *"Many weird stories are told of that time of terror, and old men still love to speak of bones turned up by the ploughshare."* **(R. Murray Gilchrist, 'The Peak District', 1911).**

Eyam is a delightful place to explore with attractive houses and interesting corners including Eyam Hall, a fine manor house built in 1671 and still the family home of the Wright family. St Lawrence's Church occupies a religious site dating back to Saxon times; note the 8th Century preaching cross in the churchyard, the finest in Derbyshire. The present church dates from the 12th Century and boasts rare 16th Century wall paintings, a cupboard made from the clothier's box that brought the plague to Eyam, a Plague Register showing the monthly death tolls, Mompesson's chair as well as Norman and Saxon fonts. In the churchyard are several interesting graves including that of Catherine, wife of William Mompesson, who died from the Plague as well as Harry Bagshaw, the famous Derbyshire and MCC cricketer, who died in 1927 and whose gravestone is adorned with bat, wickets and an umpire's hand signalling 'out'! Above a doorway is a rare sundial of 1775 that shows the time in half-hour intervals as well as the signs of the zodiac, months, longitudinal degrees and local times in several cities around the world.

Eyam was one of the first places in England to have a public water supply when a network of water troughs were erected throughout the village in 1558 supplied by springs flowing down from Eyam Edge. These provided the village water supply for over 350 years; 'eyam' comes from the Saxon words meaning 'village by the water'. This quiet village was once a hive of industrial activity with lead mining, cotton spinning, silk weaving and shoe making - the last shoe manufacturer closed in 1979. The village still boasts a Barmote Court, a relic of the lead mining era where disputes were settled and mining laws enforced. The lead mines have all closed but this peculiar court still continues, albeit on a social rather than judicial basis. The village stocks on the small green opposite Eyam Hall were once used as punishment by the Barmote Court as well as the Eyam and Stoney Middleton Association for the

Prosecution of Felons. Established in the early years of the 19th Century, this was a forerunner of the national police force where villagers took it upon themselves to appoint a constable to protect their property and offered rewards to catch offenders. This society is still going strong - you have been warned! During Victorian times Eyam was given the rather grandiose title of the 'Athens of the Peak' due to the large number of writers and poets who were either born or lived in the village, most notably Anna Steward (b. 1742) and Richard Furness (b. 1791).

From The Square in the heart of Eyam, with its old bull-ring still in situ, a narrow lane leads out of Eyam known as Lydgate. This was once the main road to Stoney Middleton where an armed 'watch and ward' guard would keep an eye on who was coming into the village during the hours of darkness. The lane passes the Lydgate Graves of plague victims George Darby and his daughter Mary set in a small enclosure.

SIR WILLIAM HILL ROAD runs across the top of Eyam Edge, one-time packhorse route, salt-road and Turnpike Road that linked Sheffield with Buxton. Some historians believe this route has Roman origins. No one is sure just who Sir William was; perhaps it was William Peverel whose built his castle overlooking the Hope Valley just after the Conquest, or Sir William Cavendish of Chatsworth or even Sir William Saville, Lord of the Manor of Eyam. The brisk climb up onto Eyam Edge to reach this old road affords wonderful views back across Eyam with the White Peak plateau rolling away into the distance.

EYAM MOOR lies to the north of Sir William Hill Road, a wonderful expanse of heather moorland with superb views in all directions. The highlight is the 'surprise' view from the brow of a bank with Stanage Edge and Higger Tor rising up above the rooftops of Hathersage and the wooded Derwent Valley far below, whilst to the north are the brooding Dark Peak moors. This moorland is littered with Bronze Age burial mounds, ancient field systems, cairns, barrows and stone circles including the famous circle known as Wet Withens.

BRETTON CLOUGH suddenly appears beneath your feet as you follow the old path down off Eyam Moor, with a wonderful view from the top of a steep scarp across this secluded valley with its trickling streams and steep hillsides cloaked in ancient woodland. Of the many deep wooded valleys that dissect Eyam Moor and Abney Moor, the wooded cleft of Bretton Clough is the most impressive. This whole area is like a huge island of hills and valleys with steep escarpments falling away on all sides into the Hope, Derwent and Bradwell valleys. Often overlooked by visitors, this is walking country par excellence! The path leads steadily down to reach the hidden beauty spot of Stoke Ford at the confluence of Abney Clough and Bretton Clough, where five old packhorse trails converge. From Stoke Ford an old track leads steadily up through the wooded side-valley of Abney Clough with its tumbling streams, mature woodland, wild flowers and rough pastures to reach the isolated hamlet of Abney.

ABNEY lies at the heart of this 'island' of wooded valleys and heather moors; secluded, peaceful and far away from the hustle and bustle of the Peak District tourist honey-pots. Situated at the head of Abney Clough and sheltered by the hills of Abney Low and Abney Moor, it consists of a single street of attractive stone-built farms and old houses. *"A lane takes you direct to Abney, a neat and clean little hamlet, as remote from the ordinary thoroughfares of mankind as any we have ever visited. Placed on a slight depression of the moor, it sees nothing around but the fields which its own industry has reclaimed and swelling uplands of sable heather."* **(M. J. B. Baddeley, 'The Peak District of Derbyshire and Neighbouring Counties', 1887).** Close by is the even smaller hamlet of Abney Grange where, in medieval times, there was a monastic farm that belonged to Rufford Abbey. The suffix 'grange' almost always identifies the site of a monastic farm. From Abney, a narrow lane leads up onto the saddle of moorland between Shatton Moor and Abney Moor at the head of Over Dale where it joins the old road across these hills known as Brough Lane.

BROUGH LANE, now just a rough track, was once a busy thoroughfare between the Hope Valley and the White Peak plateau. This is certainly a very ancient route for it follows the top of a pronounced ridge between Bradwell Dale and Over Dale thus avoiding what would have been dangerous valley routes. Perhaps this was used by the Roman legions based at the nearby fort of Navio to link up with the old road along the top of Eyam Edge, now known as Sir William Hill Road.

What is certain is that this old road crosses an ancient earthwork known as the Grey Ditch, a deep grass-covered ditch and mound that runs straight down the hillside from the curiously named Rebellion Knoll into Bradwell Dale. This mysterious earthwork was probably built in the 5th Century during the Dark Ages, which followed the demise of the Roman Empire. Following the Roman retreat, the native British people carried on much as they had done before and probably continued to live within the civilian settlement that had developed around Navio Roman fort. But soon waves of Angles and Saxons settled across the limestone plateau and valleys of the White Peak around present-day Bakewell, Tideswell and Ashbourne. However, the native British resisted this invasion and built this defensive ditch across Bradwell Dale to keep the Angles out. It would appear that the Hope Valley remained a British stronghold for many years and only became part of the burgeoning Anglo-Saxon society in the 8th Century as the Kingdom of Mercia expanded. These invading Angles who had settled across the hills and valleys of the White Peak became known as the Pecsaetne or 'hill dwellers', which is where the name of the Peak District is derived from. They replaced the ruling British elite and settled alongside the native British, rather than displacing them - rather like a change of government today. Their territory formed a buffer along part of the boundary between the kingdoms of Mercia and Northumbria, although their allegiance was towards Mercia - remember the Battle of Win and Lose hills?

The descent along Brough Lane into the Hope Valley is superb with Win Hill and Kinder Scout ahead, although there is also a bird's eye view of the cement works and associated quarries. The scale of quarrying is quite an eye-opener, although planning permissions were granted long before this area became a national park. Many people argue that these cement works, along with the many other quarries within the Peak District, are an important source of local employment and provide valuable raw materials for the construction and manufacturing industries. That said, it is hard to justify quarrying on such a scale within the setting of a national park, not to mention the creation of huge irreversible scars across the landscape. To the east of the ridge lies secluded Over Dale that cuts a deep cleft below the bulky flanks of Shatton Moor with its conspicuous transmitter mast. It is quite a surprise to find this wild valley so close to the pastoral landscape of the Hope Valley. At its head there is a dramatic waterfall, whilst further downstream its steep slopes are cloaked in deciduous woodland. Much of this valley is protected as a nature reserve by the Derbyshire Wildlife Trust as the varied terrain supports a profusion of plants and flowers.

BROUGH is a small village straddling the Roman Road of Batham Gate, which once connected the adjacent Roman fort of Navio with Aquae Arnemetiae (Buxton). Brough stands on the site of the Vicus, a civilian settlement that grew up around the fort's eastern gate with traders, craftsmen and local people attracted here by the soldiers' regular pay-packets and need for supplies. The remains of Navio Roman Fort lie in a field just to the west of Brough, the grass-covered mounds where the walls of the fort once stood clearly visible revealing its characteristic playing card shape. There are few other remains to see above ground except for a scattering of stones and also the grassy outline of the Roman road from the fort's eastern gate. There must be a wealth of stones and artefacts waiting to be discovered beneath the topsoil.

The fort has a strategic position above the confluence of Bradwell Brook and the River Noe, from which it takes its name - this river has an ancient British name, which was adopted by the Romans whilst the Anglo-Saxons later called the site 'brough' which means a defended settlement. Navio was first established in the late AD70s during the early years of the Roman invasion of Britain when Agricola, Rome's most successful Governor in Britain, pushed up through Northern England to quell the Brigantes tribes. As the legions advanced northwards, they built a network of military roads and forts from where they could keep a watchful eye on the native British. This fort was originally defended by an earthen bank topped by a wooden palisade and was in use until about 120AD when it was abandoned in favour of the Roman Empire's new frontier - Hadrian's Wall. British rebellions against the Romans meant that the fort was re-built in stone in about 150AD when it was garrisoned by 500 men of the First Cohort of Aquitanians who had been brought here from south-west France; how unlucky! The role of the fort was to guard the lead mining interests throughout the area, protect the routes through the Hope Valley and subjugate the local people. Roman roads radiated in all directions to the forts at Aquae Arnemetiae (Buxton), Ardotalia (Melandra Castle near Glossop) and Templeborough near Rotherham. Navio fort remained garrisoned for the next 200 years until the gradual collapse of the Roman Empire meant that soldiers were needed elsewhere. This was not a sudden withdrawal but a slow and steady decline for the Romans had been here for hundreds of years. They had married local people, brought up generations of families and established lives for themselves. The native British, now known as the Romano-British, had been absorbed into the Roman way of life with all that it encompassed including new farming techniques, improved infrastructure, wealth and taxation; it was not just a case of pack everything up and head back to Rome.

HOPE, from the Old English for 'valley', is a busy village situated beside the confluence of Peakshole Water and the River Noe where the Vale of Edale sweeps round to join the Hope Valley. This has always been a strategic spot with the remains of Navio Roman fort less than a mile away. The prehistoric track-way known as the Portway also came through Hope, a north to south trading route through the heart of the Peak District that once connected important settlements and sites; many of these ancient routes later developed into packhorse trails and salt roads. The history of Hope can be traced back to pre-Conquest times when it was at the heart of the Anglo-Saxon royal manor of Hope that belonged to the English king, one of many royal manors across England that were used to control and administer the country. It stretched from modern-day Buxton across to Tideswell and up into the Woodlands Valley and was subdivided into groups of villages and hamlets known as 'berewicks'. The Saxon village of Hope also boasted a church, one of only a handful of pre-Conquest churches in Derbyshire. The extensive lands that formed this Saxon royal manor were also used as a hunting forest and this pre-Conquest church served as its forest chapel. Hope was so important that it gave its name to the entire valley.

Following the Norman Conquest, this Anglo-Saxon royal manor was granted to William Peverel who formally established the Royal Forest of the Peak, a Norman hunting preserve that was administered from Peveril Castle above Castleton. This vast hunting forest was largely based upon the boundaries of the old Saxon royal manor, although it also included large tracts of land in Longdendale and around Glossop. In the early decades of Norman rule there is evidence that a small motte and bailey castle crowned by a wooden keep was built at Hope as a symbol of Norman authority within this once-important Saxon site. This castle was soon abandoned in favour of nearby Peveril Castle, which was better defended and built of stone. Some earthworks behind the Woodroffe Arms are probably the remains of this early Norman castle.

St Peter's Church dominates the village with its sturdy tower rising above the rooftops, a fine example of a broach spire. The present church dates from the 13th and 14th Centuries and has two inscribed coffin stones of former Forest huntsmen, whilst in the churchyard are a number of old crosses including the shaft of an elaborately carved Saxon cross near the south doorway. To the north of the church are the weathered remains of Eccles Cross, an ancient waymarker between Hope and Bradwell that was also used as a preaching cross; 'eccles' is an ancient British word that signifies a religious site. Look around the outside of the church to see the numerous grotesque gargoyles as well as a weathered Celtic Face set into the wall of the tower. *"A number of grotesque gargoyles, for carrying off the water from the roof, are disposed round the building, some of which, it must be confessed, hardly accord with our modern sense of decency, much less with the sacred character of the fabric they are intended to adorn."* **(James Croston, 1889).** There are also the remains of the market cross that stands atop a stepped base. Hope was granted a Market Charter in 1715 although, given its history, it was almost certainly an important trading centre for many centuries before this date. Near the church stands the Woodroffe Arms, named after an influential local family who once held the position of the King's Foresters of the Peak. The name is derived from 'wood-reeve', which means 'official of the wood'.

CASTLETON is an attractive village of grey-stone houses sheltered beneath a great arc of hills at the head of the Hope Valley with Mam Tor dominating. It is a certainly a busy place due to the combination of quaint streets, imposing castle and spectacular caverns set amidst a beautiful landscape. *"Castleton remains, as the writer first remembers it in the quiet peace of an Easter evening, a typical limestone village - a cluster of* *clean white houses, with a clear and lively brook, watched on every side, except the east, by a ring of emerald hills, just touched with mountain sternness, that stand around its calm rusticity as the hills stand round Jerusalem."* **(Joseph E. Morris, 'Peak Country', 1914).** The village developed as a planned Norman settlement in the protective shadow of Peveril Castle, which stands proudly on a dramatic promontory high above the town between the deep limestone valley of Cave Dale and the yawning chasm of Peak Cavern. It was built in 1086 by William Peverel, trusted knight of William the Conqueror, although some say he was his illegitimate son! The Hope Valley has always been of strategic and religious importance as it lies in the heart of the Peak District surrounded by mineral deposits. Our ancient ancestors recognised this, hence the hill-fort of Mam Tor as well as the prehistoric Portway route, Navio Roman fort and the Anglo-Saxon royal manor of Hope. It was no coincidence that the new Norman lords chose this site for their castle as they wanted to stamp their authority on the local people in a very visible way. That said, the castle was predominantly used to manage the lucrative local lead mines as well as the surrounding Royal Forest of the Peak. In 1155 the castle and its estate were forfeited to the Crown after Peverel's son rebelled against Henry II, who subsequently strengthened its defences with the addition of the keep, hall and gatehouse. This was the heyday of the castle when it was known as the Castle of the Peak. Henry II, King John and Henry III all visited it to hunt in the Royal Forest and in 1157 Malcolm IV, King of Scotland, visited the castle to pay homage to Henry II. In 1372 the castle passed to John of Gaunt and became part of the Duchy of Lancaster estate, although by now it was obsolete as a defensive building and was only used to administer the mines and hunting grounds. By the late 15th Century the castle had all but been abandoned.

There is much more to Castleton that meets the eye, with its jumble of lanes, attractive buildings and hidden limestone gorges. From the centre of the village, Castle Street leads up past St Edmund's Church into the attractive Market Place with its small green. This solid church dates back to the 12th Century when it was known as the Church of the Peak Castle. Despite 19th Century restoration, much of interest remains including a Norman chancel arch and 17th Century box pews. A lane known as The Stones leads to the side of the 17th Century Castleton

Hall, now a Youth Hostel, to reach Goosehill Bridge with its cluster of old cottages that once housed lead miners centuries ago. The spectacular entrance to Peak Cavern is a short riverside walk away. Castleton is also famous for its Garland Day ceremony, which takes place on Oak Apple Day (29th May). The 'king', mounted on a horse and covered from head to knee by a garland of flowers, leads a procession around the streets of Castleton that finishes at the church where the garland is hoisted to the top of the tower. The ceremony commemorates the restoration of the monarchy, although the garland of flowers has pagan origins and represents the onset of spring. A sizeable section of the old Town Ditch that once surrounded the planned Norman village can still be seen adjacent to the main car park. Planned settlements such as this were almost always associated with castles and were built as income generators for the lords of the castle who offered a relatively safe place for craftsmen and traders to live and work but charged taxes and market tolls for the privilege. The layout of this Norman settlement can still be seen with its grid pattern of streets surrounding the market place and church.

Castleton is situated at the point where the White Peak limestone meets the Dark Peak gritstone. The limestone hills to the west and south were formed 350 million years ago as a coral reef in a warm tropical sea. Since Roman times, these hills have been mined for lead and the semi-precious Blue John stone, a unique type of fluorspar. Levels were driven into the hillsides and natural limestone caves opened up, four of which can be visited today as show caves including Peak Cavern, Speedwell Cavern, Treak Cliff Cavern and Blue John Cavern. A tour of the Blue John Cavern reveals a labyrinth of natural caverns as well as old mine workings where veins of Blue John can be seen sandwiched between the limestone rock. These veins are still worked by miners and the Blue John is crafted into jewellery and ornaments. Blue John is only found in the hill of Treak Cliff; a purple, yellow and white-banded fluorspar that got its name from the French words 'bleu jaune' meaning blue and yellow. It is said that Blue John vases were found amongst the ruins of Pompeii, although it was particularly popular in Georgian and Victorian times. Nearby is Treak Cliff Cavern, which also has rich deposits of Blue John amongst a cave system that is renowned for its stalactites and stalagmites. Situated at the foot of Winnats Pass, Speedwell Cavern involves a boat journey along a flooded level through the workings of a 200-year-old lead mine to reach underground cave and river systems. Peak Cavern is the final show cave, hidden in a dramatic gorge behind Castleton. The entrance to this cavern is awe-inspiring, a huge yawning hole that so frightened our ancestors that they thought it was the entrance to hell, hence its other name of the Devil's Arse! *"Behind the ridge, a deep ravine called Cave Dale from the head of the village street goes winding and narrowing into slopes of rock and turf, then some way up gives a striking view of the Castle. The other face of the hill is deeply pierced by the Peak Cavern, so called par excellence; and it naturally took a by-title from the devil: liberal shepherds give us a grosser name, in our day quite unmentionable to ears polite."* **(A. R. Hope Moncrieff, 1908).** This is the largest cave entrance in the British Isles, where a community of ropemakers once lived and worked during the 18th and 19th Centuries making ropes for the local lead mines, as the damp atmosphere provided perfect conditions. The last of Castleton's ropemakers retired in 1973. The tour takes you for half a mile deep underground through the Lumbago walk and into the Great Cave where you can see the Orchestral Gallery and Roger Rain's House. Beyond the show cave lie thirteen miles of caves that link up with Speedwell Cavern and Titan.

Castleton

CASTLETON
to
HAYFIELD

✦

"Thoughts run deep in wild places, and the old packhorse route between Edale and Hayfield is one such place. For many centuries people have walked this way, toiling up the steep slopes, braving biting winds and stinging rain. Before the days of maps and guidebooks, it would have come as great relief and reassurance to see the crudely fashioned Edale Cross at the top of the pass giving both geographical and spiritual guidance across these dangerous hills. Your companions, now as then, are tumbling streams, distant vistas and towering slopes that are crowned by massive outcrops fashioned by nature into weird and wonderful shapes. Trade and industry was carried out on foot for many thousands of years; these old packhorse routes were the motorways of their day. This tradition is all but lost, but there is something to be said for travelling slowly on foot. It allows time to think, to understand yourself and appraise your place in the natural world around. For countless generations, we travelled on foot from village to village; this walk through the Peak District is simply continuing that tradition."

Mark Reid
October 2006

WALK INFORMATION

· ·

Points of interest: A castle perched upon high, the Shivering Mountain, a walk across the Great Ridge, a classic walkers' pub, the 'island valley', in the footsteps of jaggers, climbing the stairway to heaven, a medieval wayside cross and a superb descent along an old packhorse trail.

Distance:

Castleton to Edale		5.5 miles
Edale to Hayfield		6 miles
Total		11.5 miles

Time: Allow 5 - 6 hours

Terrain: From Castleton, a path heads up through Cave Dale (steep and rocky) to join a stony track which is followed to reach the road below Mam Tor. There is then a steep climb along a grassy/stone-pitched path up onto the summit of Mam Tor (exposed to the elements). From Mam Tor, a flagged path follows the crest of the Great Ridge to Hollins Cross from where a rough path drops steeply down to join a track beside Hollins Farm which is followed down to join the road through the Vale of Edale. Field paths then lead to Grindsbrook Booth (Edale). From Edale, field paths (flagged in places) head up through the valley to Upper Booth from where a lane/track leads steadily up alongside the River Noe passing Lee Farm to reach a packhorse bridge. There is then a steep climb up Jacob's Ladder (stone-pitched path). From the top of Jacob's Ladder, a stony track climbs up to Edale Cross at the top of the pass, from where the track drops steadily down into the Upper Sett Valley to join a farm lane.

Clear woodland paths then lead into Hayfield. *This walk involves a number of steep sections. Keep to the path across the top of Mam Tor - sheer cliffs on its south-eastern edge. Take care crossing the roads at the foot of Mam Tor and through Edale. Limestone is slippery when wet.*

Ascents:	Mam Tor:	517 metres
	Edale Cross:	541 metres

Viewpoints: Cave Dale looking towards Peveril Castle. Mam Tor with views across the Hope Valley and Vale of Edale. The descent from Hollins Cross looking across the Vale of Edale. Kinder Scout from Jacob's Ladder. Far-reaching views during the descent from Edale Cross across the Upper Sett Valley.

FACILITIES

. . . .

Castleton	Inn / B&B / Shop / PO / Café / Bus / Phone / Toilets / Info / YH / Camp
Edale	Inn / B&B / Shop / PO / Café / Bus / Train / Phone / Toilets / Info / YH / Camp
Upper Booth	Café / Phone / Camp
Hayfield	Inn / B&B / Shop / PO / Café / Bus / Phone / Toilets / Info / Camp

ROUTE DESCRIPTION

. . . .

(Map Sixteen)

From the small triangular green in Castleton Market Place head up along the road out of the top corner of the Market Place along Bargate then, where the road bends round to the left after a short distance (Pindale Road), turn right along a path (SP 'Cave Dale'). Follow this up out of the village and through a narrow limestone gorge after a few paces to reach a gate at the bottom of Cave Dale. Head through the gate and follow the rocky path straight on, which soon opens out into Cave Dale - carry straight on along the path heading up through the dry limestone valley (Peveril Castle up to your right), passing caves then climbing quite steeply up through a narrow rocky section to reach a gateway in a wall at the top of this rocky section. Carry straight on along the clear path alongside the wall on your right gradually heading up through the valley for 0.75 miles to reach a bridlegate in a wall across your path near the head of the valley. After the bridlegate, carry straight on up through the shallow head of the valley (tumbledown wall on your left) to soon reach another bridlegate in a wall, after which carry straight on for approx. 50 yards where you follow the wide grassy path bearing to the left up across the hillside out of the head of the valley. This path soon levels out and leads on across the large, open field bearing slightly to the right to join the wall on your right which you follow to quickly reach a gate where you head straight on along a short section of enclosed track to quickly reach another gate/wall-stile that leads onto a crossroads of tracks. Turn right along the enclosed track and follow this for approx. 250 yards then, where it forks, take the enclosed track to the right and follow this for just under 0.5 miles to reach a gate across the track, after which carry straight on to soon reach the entrance driveway towards Rowter Farm (track becomes a metalled lane). Carry straight on along the lane for just under 0.5 miles to reach a road.

At the road, take the FP opposite to the right through a gate (SP) and follow the rough track straight on alongside the wall on your left then, where this wall bends away, carry straight on along the rough track to reach the road (former A625) at the foot of Mam Tor. At the road, take the bridlegate opposite to the left and follow the grassy path straight on heading steeply up to reach a small gate at the top of the field, after which head up some steps to reach the road at Mam Nick (just below Mam Tor). As you reach the road, take the FP immediately to your right through the bridlegate and follow the steps/flagged path climbing steeply up onto the summit of Mam Tor (Trig Point). At the summit, carry straight on along the stone-flagged path *(keep to the path)* steadily dropping down from the summit then gradually curving round to the right following the path along the top of the Great Ridge for 0.75 miles to reach a 'crossroads' of paths at Hollins Cross (circular stone memorial) at the bottom of the 'saddle' of land between Mam Tor and Barker Bank (just before the ridge climbs up onto Barker Bank).

At Hollins Cross, turn left off the ridge then immediately left again where the path forks and follow this rough, wide path slanting down across the hillside into the Vale of Edale. Follow this path down then, where it forks after about 150 yards, follow the right-hand path heading quite steeply down across the hillside to reach a small gate in a wall 50 yards to the left of Hollins Farm. Head though the gate and drop down to join the farm track, which you follow to the left down passing some barns then down across a field to reach a bridge across the River Noe. Continue along the track over the bridge then, as you approach the road, head up through the small gate ahead to join the road. At the road, take the FP opposite (SP) and walk up the field alongside the wall on your left then, three-quarters of the way up the field, head left through a squeeze-stile. After the squeeze-stile, head diagonally to the right across the field to join a grassy track that leads beneath a railway bridge, after which head straight on along the grassy track up to reach a gate in the field corner. Do not head through this gate but turn left immediately before it through a squeeze-stile then bear right across the field to reach another stile just to the right of a barn. After this stile, follow the path straight on across the field (flagged at first) to join a fence/wooded banks of Grinds Brook (stream) on your left which you follow up to soon reach a gate to your left and a metalled lane. Head through this gate and follow the lane over a bridge across Grinds Brook immediately after which follow the FP to the right up through woodland to join the road through Grindsbrook Booth (Edale) opposite Edale Church. Turn right along the road to reach the Old Nag's Head in the heart of the village.

(Map Seventeen)

Just as you reach the Old Nag's Head turn left along a rough track (SP 'Pennine Way, Upper Booth') passing in front of an old stone house with mullion windows and then some farm buildings then carry straight on along an enclosed tree-shaded path alongside a stream on your right leaving Grindsbrook Booth behind. Follow this clear path gently rising up for 0.25 miles to reach the top of the enclosed path/stream where you turn left through a small gate in a fence (SP 'Pennine Way, Upper Booth'). Follow the flagged path straight on gently rising up across four fields through a succession of wall-gates, after which the path levels out and leads straight on across the hillside (Vale of Edale sweeping away to your left) to reach a small wall-gate beside some pine trees. Head through the wall-gate and carry straight on gently rising up (waymarker 'PW via Jacob's Ladder') onto a spur of land (landslip) where you continue straight on to soon reach another wall-gate at the top of the rise. After this wall-gate, follow the path bearing to the right down across the hillocky hillside to reach a stile over a fence, after which head left down the hillside alongside a fence on your left at first then, where this fence/wall bends away (ruinous barn), carry on down through a small gate in a fence then bear slightly to the right down through two old stone gateposts and down to reach a gate in the bottom field corner that leads onto an enclosed track. Follow this track straight on then, as you reach the houses/farm buildings at Upper Booth, follow the track to the left down through the yard of Upper Booth Farm to reach a road (opposite the phone box).

Turn right along the road (SP 'Pennine Way, Jacob's Ladder') down over a bridge across Crowden Brook then follow this road straight on for 0.5 miles to reach Lee House Farm. Head straight on through the farmyard (information barn) along the stony track to reach a gate at the far end of the farmyard, after which carry straight on along the track heading gradually up through the valley, with the River Noe just to your left, for 0.75 miles to reach the packhorse bridge across the Noe at the foot of Jacob's Ladder (stone-pitched path). Cross the packhorse bridge, after which follow the stone-pitched path to the right (National Trust sign 'Jacob's Ladder') climbing steeply up Jacob's Ladder to reach a large cairn and a junction of paths at the top of the steep climb. Follow the clear, rocky track to the right climbing steadily up for 0.5 miles to reach a gate across the track set in a wall corner. Head through the gate (ignore

Pennine Way to the right) and follow the track straight on alongside a wall on your right for a further 0.25 miles up to reach a gateway in a wall across the track at the top of the pass, with Edale Cross set in a small enclosure just beyond.

(Map Eighteen)

Carry straight on along the track passing Edale Cross and follow this track steadily dropping down alongside a wall on your right to reach a gate across the track after just over 0.5 miles where you carry straight on along the track for a further 400 yards to reach a second gate across the track where the wall ends on your right (National Trust sign 'Kinder Estate'). Head through the gate and follow the track down across a field, enclosed by fences, to reach a stile beside a gate at the bottom of the field (SP 'Hayfield') after which follow the enclosed stony track straight on down (wall on your right) to reach another gate (track becomes a metalled lane). Head through this gate and follow the lane straight on for a few paces down to reach a junction of lanes where you head to the right over a bridge across Coldwell Clough and follow this lane down with the stream on your left to reach Coldwell Clough Farm. Carry straight on along the lane down through Coldwell Clough then curving round to the right to join the banks of the River Sett (Upper Sett Valley) where you carry straight on to soon reach a fork in the lane - follow the left-hand lane through a gate and over a bridge across the River Sett.

After the bridge, carry straight on along the lane climbing up and curving gently up to the right *(ignore the first two tracks/BW off to the left)* then, where the lane levels out, take the track branching up to the left (SP 'Pennine Bridleway Hayfield'). Follow this track climbing up to reach a bridlegate in a wall, after which head straight on along the level path (waymarker 'PBW') alongside a wall and bottom edge of Elle Bank Wood on your left. The path curves round to the left then drops down to the right passing to the left side of Stones House after which the path drops steadily down (still heading along the bottom edge of Elle Bank Wood) then levels out and enters the woodland (ignore FP to right into the campsite). Carry straight on along the path through woodland (SP

'Hayfield') down to join a riverside path (River Sett). Follow this riverside path straight on to quickly join a road beside a row of terraced houses *(FB to right leads up to Sportsman Inn)*, where you carry straight on along this road (river to your right) heading into Hayfield to join the top of Church Street where you turn right down into the village centre.

Cave Dale

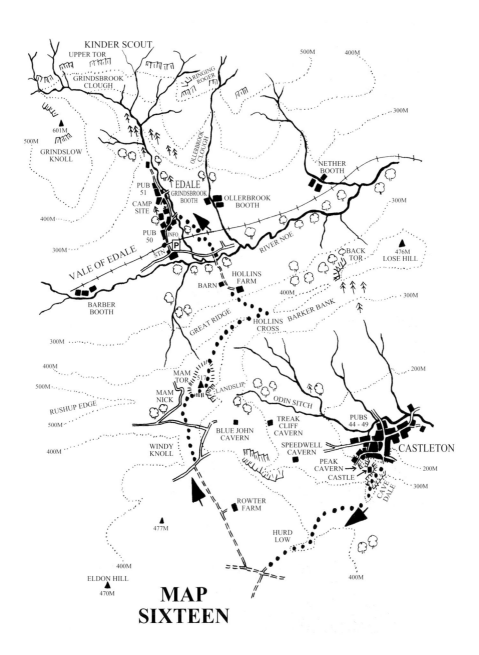

MAP
SIXTEEN

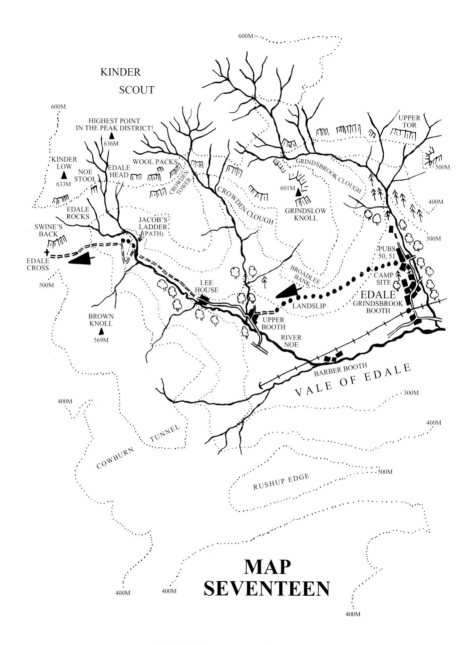

KINDER

SCOUT

600M

HIGHEST POINT
IN THE PEAK DISTRICT!

636M

KINDER
LOW

NOE
STOOL

633M

EDALE
HEAD

WOOL PACKS

CROWDEN TOWER

EDALE
ROCKS

JACOB'S
LADDER
(PATH)

CROWDEN CLOUGH

CROWDEN CLOUGH

601M

GRINDSBROOK CLOUGH

GRINDSLOW
KNOLL

UPPER
TOR

500M

400M

SWINE'S
BACK

EDALE
CROSS

500M

LEE
HOUSE

BROADLEE
BANK

LANDSLIP

300M

PUBS
50, 51

CAMP
SITE

EDALE
GRINDSBROOK
BOOTH

BROWN
KNOLL

569M

UPPER
BOOTH

RIVER
NOE

BARBER BOOTH

VALE OF EDALE

400M

300M

400M

COWBURN TUNNEL

RUSHUP EDGE

500M

MAP
SEVENTEEN

400M

400M

400M

MAP
EIGHTEEN

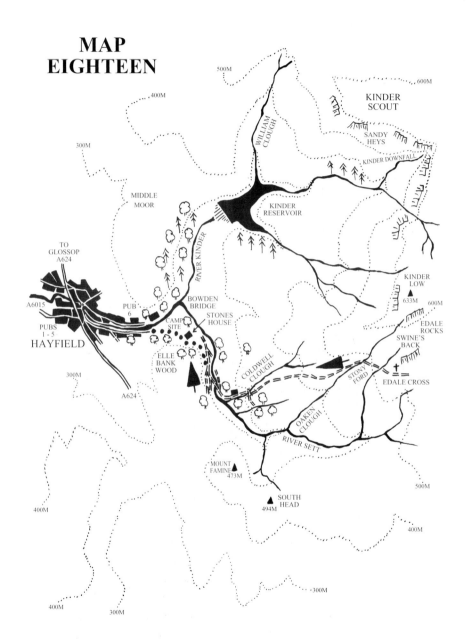

CAVE DALE is a spectacular limestone valley that can be found just off Castleton's Market Place, its narrow entrance passageway hidden behind some cottages. This craggy, steep-sided dry valley sweeps up beneath the ramparts of Peveril Castle before a final pull up through a narrow rocky cleft reveals a superb retrospective view of the castle perched precariously above the brink. There is some dispute as to how this valley was formed; a collapsed cave system, the action of glacial meltwaters or the remains of an underwater channel formed when this whole area was submerged beneath a tropical sea some 350 million years ago. As you walk up through Cave Dale, you are actually walking on the roof of Peak Cavern as well as a labyrinth of other smaller caves. Indeed, in 1999 the UK's largest natural cave chamber was discovered near Cave Dale by cavers exploring the system between Peak Cavern and Speedwell Cavern. Known as Titan, this vast cavern has a vertical depth of 464-ft.

MAM TOR - the Mother Mountain - is ringed by a prehistoric hill-fort, built by the native Celtic tribes some 3,000 years ago during the Iron Age, although there are two Bronze Age burial mounds on its summit that possibly date back as far as 6,000 years. There was a sizeable settlement within these ramparts with at least seventy hut circles cut into the slopes of Mam Tor. Hill-forts such as this were not solely built for defence but were a bold statement of status and power by the local chieftain. They often had religious significance and were also used as a social centre for meetings and trade; indeed, the prehistoric route known as the Portway led from the East Midlands through the heart of the Peak District to Mam Tor. Originally, the earth ramparts would have been capped by timber palisades, later replaced by stone walls - the footpath up to its summit from Mam Nick follows the prehistoric pathway through the original entrance.

Mam Tor is also known as the 'shivering mountain' as the unstable layers of shales and gritstone have been slipping away over thousands of years causing huge landslides. A massive landslide many hundreds, if not thousands, of years ago caused its eastern face to completely fall away whilst, more recently, the main A625 between Sheffield and Chapel-en-le-Frith was swept away in 1979 - and the hillside is still moving at around 9cm a year. Mam Tor stands at the dividing point between the

Dark and White Peak, where the limestone plateau and valleys of the White Peak meet the shales and gritstones of the Dark Peak - look closely and you will notice the change in vegetation as you approach the foot of Mam Tor. This is geology at its best. The views from its summit are extensive with the Hope Valley sweeping away to the east, the Vale of Edale to the north framed by the towering slopes of Kinder Scout and the Great Ridge curving round in an arc towards the conical peak of Lose Hill on its eastern nab. It is easy to see why our ancient ancestors chose this hill for such an important spiritual site. A word of caution though - keep to the path across the summit as there are sheer cliffs just to the east caused by the massive landslip. *"The ridge walk from Mam Tor to Back Tor and Lose Hill is perhaps the pleasantest hill excursion in Derbyshire, for the simple reason that it is a real ridge - in places almost meriting the term razor-edge - and on that account commands an extensive prospect on both sides, - of Edale on the left and Hope Dale on the right, two of the finest of the Derbyshire valleys."* **(M. J. B. Baddeley, 'The Peak District of Derbyshire and Neighbouring Counties', 1887).**

HOLLINS CROSS marks an important junction of old footways and packhorse routes between Castleton and the Vale of Edale via the 'saddle' of land between Mam Tor and Barker Bank along the Great Ridge. In medieval times this busy junction of routes would have been marked by a wayside cross but is now graced by a circular stone-built memorial. Many centuries ago, this was also the 'coffin route' taken by funeral processions from the Vale of Edale to bury their dead in the churchyard at Castleton as there was no church in the Vale of Edale. In 1633 a small chapel was built at Grindsbrook Booth (Edale), replaced by the present Edale Church in 1885, which thankfully meant no more arduous journeys across the Great Ridge carrying a coffin!

THE VALE OF EDALE was once known as the 'island valley' for it is hemmed in by the towering escarpment of Kinder Scout to the north and the rounded hills of Mam Tor and the Great Ridge to the south. For centuries, it was virtually cut off from the outside world accessible only on foot along old packhorse routes until the railway arrived in the late 19th Century. Known affectionately as the 'ramblers' railway', this popular railway links Sheffield with Manchester and heads through the heart of the Vale of Edale before entering the two-mile long Cowburn Tunnel that burrows 800-ft beneath the moorland ridge between Brown Knoll and Rushup Edge. Along the valley floor are five clusters of farms and cottages known locally as booths although the largest of these, Grindsbrook Booth, is more commonly called Edale. The word 'booth' is derived from an old Scandinavian word for a shepherd's shelter. They were originally established as cattle farms sometime after the Norman Conquest when this whole area fell within the boundaries of the Royal Forest of the Peak. From humble beginnings, they have grown into picturesque villages. The 'booths' all shelter below the towering escarpment of Kinder Scout that rises high above, an awe-inspiring landscape of wild moorland, jagged rocks and deep cloughs. The Vale of Edale is a classic Pennine valley with its patchwork of fields, drystone walls, wooded ravines and tumbling streams, scattered stone-built farmsteads and lovely villages all of which are hemmed in by ever-watching moors and hills. It is these hills that draw outdoor enthusiasts to this secluded valley in their thousands; Edale lies on the threshold of some of the finest and most challenging walking country in England.

The River Noe flows through this beautiful valley. From its source high on the Kinder Scout plateau near the solitary gritstone outcrop known as the Noe Stool, the River Noe gathers peaty waters from a myriad of deep groughs before tumbling down from the plateau through a steep clough. The infant river skirts the foot of Jacob's Ladder before it charts a more leisurely course to reach the hamlet of Upper Booth. The river quickly matures and meanders through the valley passing the remaining four 'booths', all located on the sunnier north bank of the river. Beyond Nether Booth, the river swings southwards hemmed in by the Win Hill ridge, with road and railway close companions, to reach its confluence with Peakshole Water just to the east of Hope where it becomes the Hope Valley. *"... a secluded valley with a tiny rivulet flowing through its midst; and the quaintly-named hamlets of Over Booth, Nether Booth, Barber Booth, and Lady Booth look down from the steep bluffs and tufted slopes upon a miniature old church, with a tiny bell-cot, all looking so primitive and "unimproved" that you might fancy the world to have stood still for centuries."* (**James Croston, "On Foot through The Peak", 1889**).

GRINDSBROOK BOOTH, more popularly known as Edale, is known throughout the country for one thing - walking. Edale, or more precisely the Old Nag's Head, marks the official starting point of the Pennine Way, Britain's first National Trail. In 1935 Tom Stephenson, access campaigner and soon-to-be secretary of the Ramblers Association, wrote an article in the Daily Herald entitled 'Wanted: A Long Green Trail' where he championed the idea of a long trek across the backbone of Britain. At that time, much of the open country of the high Pennines was out of bounds for walkers, although the campaign to gain access to these forbidden hills was gathering pace. Thirty years later the Pennine Way officially opened, tracing a 268-mile route across the roof of the Pennines from Edale to Kirk Yetholm in the Scottish Borders. *"The fine cleft into Kinderscout behind is forbidden ground, unless during the winter, when the few grouse need not be so jealously guarded from disturbance."* **(A. R. Hope Moncrieff, 'The Peak Country', 1908)**

As you walk along the narrow road through the heart of the village towards the Old Nag's Head, excitement and trepidation builds as the escarpment of Kinder Scout's southern rim looms high above the rooftops rising over 600 metres above sea level in an almost sheer wall of slopes punctuated by shattered gritstone outcrops. The outcrops of Grindslow Knoll, Upper Tor and Ringer Roger dominate, crowning the edge of the deep ravine of Grindsbrook Clough that cuts a huge cleft into the plateau behind the village. The name of Ringing Roger is thought to be derived from the French word for rocks as the wind often howls through these outcrops, although a story is told of a local lad called Roger who was a keen bell-ringer and used to walk up to these outcrops to practice as the acoustics were just right for his bells! In the heart of the village is the Moorland Centre, a new flagship visitor and learning centre and home to the Moors for the Future Partnership. This project aims to restore and conserve the fragile moorland landscape through education, interpretation, research and conservation. By increasing awareness and understanding, coupled with footpath repairs and moorland restoration, it is hoped that the future of these important moorland landscapes can be secured. The Peak District moorlands, including Kinder Scout, are the most visited moorland areas in the world and the Moors for the Future Partnership is the biggest upland conservation project in Britain. The Moorland Centre is housed in an eco-friendly building with an insulating turf roof, waterfall and ground source heating system.

Several important packhorse trails once converged at Grindsbrook Booth, indeed, just down to the side of the Old Nag's Head is a stone packhorse bridge that spans Grinds Brook. This classic pub dates back to 1577 and was built to provide refreshment for travellers and tradesmen; indeed, its name comes from the packhorses that would often be lined up outside waiting for their 'jaggers'. Their preferred horses were either Galloway or the German Jaeger breeds, and so the men leading these packhorse trains became known as jaggers after their horses. Between the 16th and 19th Centuries these packhorse routes were the arterial routes of England, along which raw materials such as salt, coal, lead and iron as well as finished goods were carried. The growth of the railway network during the 19th Century heralded their terminal decline. To the west of Grindsbrook Booth, this old packhorse route initially follows an old tree-shaded track known as Peat Lane that was once used by villagers to bring sods of dried peat down from Kinder Scout to be used as fuel. Beyond the top of this old lane, the stone-flagged path gently rises up to reach the huge landslip at the foot of Broadlee Bank where unstable layers of shales sandwiched between the gritstones have slid away, similar to the massive landslips on the flanks of Mam Tor across the valley.

UPPER BOOTH is a delightful cluster of cottages and farm buildings situated just above the wooded ravine of Crowden Clough, which comes headlong down from the wilds of Edale Moor. The walk passes through the yard of Upper Booth Farm, a working farm that forms part of the National Trust's High Peak estate. It is an excellent example of rural diversification with a campsite, camping barn and seasonal café that benefits from the Pennine Way, and now The Inn Way, which pass through its farmyard. From Upper Booth, a lane leads up to reach Lee Farm where the lane becomes a track. The attractive range of farm buildings include a National Trust information barn and shelter. Little appears to have changed here for centuries and it is easy to imagine trains of thirty to forty packhorses plodding nose to tail laden with goods and bells jangling, being led by a weather-beaten jagger having just crossed the high moors from Hayfield. *"The traveller down Edale, by the way, should keep a sharp look-out for dogs, who, as usual in the remote corners of the land, are less partial to new faces and more inquisitive as to strange legs than in populous parts."* **(M. J. B. Baddeley, 1887).**

Beyond Lee Farm, the track continues climbing steadily into the upper reaches of the Vale of Edale alongside the infant River Noe. Ahead, the towering hills of Kinder Scout and Brown Knoll crowd in presenting a seemingly impenetrable barrier, their sheer flanks rising up on all sides, deeply fissured by cloughs with silhouetted gritstone outcrops punctuating the crest of the escarpment. The climb across these hills over to Hayfield looks more daunting than it actually is. Honestly!

Upper Booth

JACOB'S LADDER is renowned throughout the walking world as the first ascent along the Pennine Way and a famous route up onto Kinder Scout. From the old packhorse bridge across the infant River Noe, an exciting pitched-stone path leads steeply up out of the upper reaches of the Vale of Edale. This path takes its name from Jacob Marshall, an 18th Century local man who farmed at Edale Head and lived in the now ruinous Youngate farmhouse. According to folklore, Jacob Marshall cut these steps into the hillside to create a more direct route for the jagger men to climb, leaving their packhorses to walk up the original (and longer) zig-zagging route that can still be seen just to the left. This short-cut meant that the jaggers could have a well-earned rest at the top waiting for their horses to catch up! The narrow packhorse bridge at the foot of Jacob's Ladder, known locally as Youngate Bridge, is a delightful place to rest weary legs before the steep climb, with grassy riverbanks and a series of small waterfalls close by.

Edale Cross

EDALE CROSS stands at the highest point (541 metres) along the old packhorse route between Cheshire and Yorkshire. This cross is thought to date back to Norman times and was originally erected in 1157 to mark the boundary of monastic lands of Basingwerke Abbey near Holywell who had been granted the Manor of Glossop by Henry II. This whole area formed part of the Royal Forest of the Peak and Edale Cross also marked the meeting point of three ward boundaries within this vast Norman hunting preserve. Later, this ancient cross would have also acted as a wayside guidepost along the packhorse route, providing reassurance and guidance to countless travellers who came this way across the southern shoulder of Kinder Scout. Back then, there were no walls or boundaries just a vast expanse of open moorland that presented many dangers to travellers and so a wayside cross would have offered both spiritual and geographical guidance. From here, it's downhill all the way to Hayfield, a wonderful way to end this walk with a glorious landscape of green hills and deep valleys as far as the eye can see.

THE RIVER SETT rises amongst the peat hags just to the south of Edale Cross on the flanks of Brown Knoll (569 metres). Fed by numerous streams, the infant waters of this river soon tumble down through a deeply incised clough skirting beneath the prominent hills of South Head and Mount Famine which dominate the Upper Sett Valley. Hidden away in a wooded ravine is the isolated Coldwell Clough Farm, a fine example of an early 19th Century farmhouse that has recently been acquired by the National Trust as part of their High Peak estate. This estate covers a vast swathe of moorland throughout the Dark Peak that are owned, managed and protected by the National Trust including Kinder Scout, Bleaklow, Derwent Moors and Mam Tor, which together form some of the most important and sensitive upland landscape in Britain. Below Coldwell Clough Farm, the track soon joins the banks of the River Sett, which now flows northwards through a beautiful valley before its confluence with the River Kinder at Bowden Bridge. The River Sett then turns westwards, flowing through Hayfield and down through the Sett Valley to swell the waters of the River Goyt at New Mills.

The final mile or so of The Inn Way follows an old bridleway that skirts below Elle Bank Wood with fine views across the Upper Sett Valley towards Middle Moor and White Brow above Kinder Reservoir where this walk began some six days ago. The end of the walk is fast approaching; time to reminisce and to reflect on what you have just achieved. The walk may be coming to an end but the journey through the Peak District will continue for the rest of your life. As a true brother of the boot, this walk will kindle a lifelong and intimate relationship with the heather-clad moors, green rounded hills, lush limestone valleys, neat villages and cosy pubs, fascinating history, impressive geology and the friendly people of the Peak District. It did with me.

BIBLIOGRAPHY

The following books are listed as follows: author, title, date first published and publisher.

M. J. B. Baddeley, 'The Peak District of Derbyshire and Neighbouring Counties', 1887, Dulau & Co.

James Croston, 'On Foot through The Peak', 1889, John Heywood & Co.

John Derry (author), revised by G. H. B. Ward, 'Across the Derbyshire Moors', 1904 (revised 1939), Sheffield Telegraph & Star Ltd.

A. R. Hope Moncrieff, 'The Peak Country', 1908, A & C Black.

R. Murray Gilchrist, 'The Peak District', 1911, Blackie & Son Ltd.

Jospeh E. Morris, 'Peak Country', 1914, A & C Black.

Patrick Monkhouse, 'On Foot in the Peak', 1932, A. Maclehose & Co.

Arthur Mee, 'Derbyshire', 1937, Hodder & Stoughton Ltd.

C. E. M. Joad (Editor), 'The English Counties', 1949, Odhams Press Ltd.

R. Redfern, 'Rambles in Peakland', 1965, Robert Hale.

N. Batley & B. James; John Hadfield (Editor), 'The Shell Guide to England - the North Midlands', 1970, Michael Joseph.

Various, 'Walks in the Derbyshire Dales', 1973, Derbyshire Countryside Ltd.

K. C. Edwards, 'The Peak District', 1973, Collins.

Arkwright Society, 'Caudwell's Mill, Rowsley', 1974, G. C. Brittain & Sons Ltd.

Mark Richards, 'High Peak Walks, 1982, Cicerone.

Mark Richards, 'White Peak Walks: The Northern Dales', 1985, Cicerone.

Derek Gibling (Vicar), 'Youlgreave Parish Church; A Guide', 1987, G. C. Brittain & Sons Ltd.

Lindsey Porter, 'The Peak District', 1989, David & Charles.

L. Porter 'The Visitor's Guide to the Peak District', 1989, Moorland Publishing Ltd.

Beric Morley, 'Peveril Castle', 1990, English Heritage.

L. Lumsdon & M. Smith, 'Pub Walks in the Peak District: White Peak', 1991, Sigma Leisure.

W. A. Poucher, 'Peak & Pennine Country', 1991, Constable.

Jim Gracie, 'Hidden Places of the Peak District', 1991, Travel Publishing.

R & M Freethy, 'Getting to know the Peak District', 1992, Printwise Publications.

Mike Harding, 'Walking the Peak and Pennines', 1992, Michael Joseph.

B. Conduit & K. Borman, 'Peak District Walks', 1993, Jarrold Publishing.

J & A Nuttall, 'Walker's Companion: Peak District', 1994, Ward Lock.

Robert Innes-Smith, 'Castleton and its Caves', 1994, Derbyshire Countryside Ltd.

Tony Hopkins, 'The Peak District', 1996, AA Publishing.

Charles Hurt, 'On Foot in the Peak District', 1996, David & Charles.

J. Barnatt & K. Smith, 'The Peak District: Landscapes through time', 1997, English Heritage.

Paul Hannon, 'Walking Country: Northern Peak', 1997, Hillside Publications.

Paul Hannon, 'Walking Country: Central Peak', 1997, Hillside Publications.

Paul Hannon, 'Walking Country: Eastern Peak', 1997, Hillside Publications.

Andrew McCloy, 'Walking in Youlgrave', 1998, Benchmark Books.

Brian Spencer, 'Visitor's Guide: Peak District', 1999, Visitor's Guides Ltd.

L. Porter 'Southern Peak District', 1999, Landmark Publishing Ltd.

N. Aitkenhead & A. Dennis, 'Holiday Geology Map: Peak District', 1999, British Geological Survey.

R. Smith, 'The Peak District, the Official National Park Guide', 2000, Pevensey Guides.

R. Smith. 'Collins Rambler's Guide: Peak District', 2001, Harper Collins.

Andrew McCloy, 'The Peak District Pub Guide', 2002, Johnson Publishing.

Various, '50 Walks in the Peak District', 2002, AA Publishing.

M. Hulbert & P. Miles, 'The Parish Church of St Michael and All Angels Hathersage', 2003, Hathersage Parochial Church Council.

K. Borman, 'Jarrold Short Walks; the Peak District', 2004, Jarrold Publishing.

L. Lumsdon & M. Smith, 'Pub Walks in the Peak District: Dark Peak', 2004, Sigma Leisure.

Various, 'Pub Walks & Cycle Rides; The Peak District', 2005, AA Publishing.

Roger Protz (Editor), 'Good Beer Guide', 2006, CAMRA.

Simon Kirwam, 'Peak District Villages', 2006, Myriad Books.

Canon Martin F. H. Hulbert, 'Bishop Pursglove of Tideswell, date unknown, Parochial Church Council of Tideswell.

Hayfield Civic Trust, 'Hayfield History Trail', date unknown.

The Inn Way...to the Peak District

LOG BOOK

. . . .

"Drinking in the scenery"

Visit as many of the fifty-one pubs along The Inn Way...to the Peak District as possible and keep a record of your progress with this Log Book.

Send your completed Log Book to the address below to receive your free 'Inn Way Certificate' (please include an A4 SAE as well as your name and address, we will return this Log Book with your certificate). Photocopies of this Log Book will not be accepted.

'The Inn Way' Merchandise & Gifts

If you would like to purchase an 'Inn Way Certificate' then please write to us for a copy of 'The Inn Way' colour brochure:

We produce a range of walking guidebooks as well as a selection of quality merchandise and gift items including 'Inn Way' branded outdoor fleeces, polo shirts, performance T-shirts, beenie hats, glass beer tankards, fabric badges, postcards featuring the pen and ink drawings from the books plus much more...

InnWay Publications
102 LEEDS ROAD
HARROGATE
HG2 8HB

www.innway.co.uk

LOG BOOK

. . . .

Day One   **Time of visit Date Remarks**

1. Royal Hotel, Hayfield

2. Bull's Head, Hayfield

3. George Hotel, Hayfield

4. Kinder Lodge, Hayfield

5. Packhorse, Hayfield

6. Sportsman, Hayfield

7. Snake Pass Inn

8. Yorkshire Bridge Inn

9. Anglers Rest, Bamford

10. Ye Derwent Hotel, Bamford

11. Scotsmans Pack, Hathersage

12. George Hotel, Hathersage

13. Little John Inn, Hathersage

14. Plough Inn, Leadmill Bridge

15. Millstone Country Inn, Hathersage Booths

Day Two

16. Fox House Inn, Longshaw

17. Grouse Inn, Froggatt Edge

18. Devonshire Arms, Baslow

19. Rowley's Restaurant and Bar, Baslow

20. Rutland Arms, Baslow

21. Wheatsheaf Hotel, Baslow

Day Three

22. Devonshire Arms, Beeley

23. Grouse & Claret, Rowsley

24. Peacock, Rowsley

25. Flying Childers, Stanton in Peak

26. Red Lion, Birchover

27. Druid Inn, Birchover

28. Bull's Head Hotel, Youlgrave

29. Farmyard Inn, Youlgrave

30. George Hotel, Youlgrave

Day Four

31. Bull's Head, Monyash

32. Cock and Pullet, Sheldon

33. Stables Bar (Monsal Head Hotel)

34. The Star, Tideswell

35. George Hotel, Tideswell

36. Horse & Jockey, Tideswell

Day Five

37. Red Lion, Litton

38. Three Stags Heads, Wardlow Mires

39. Bull's Head Inn, Foolow

40. Miners' Arms, Eyam

41. Travellers Rest, Brough

42. Old Hall, Hope

43. Woodroffe Arms, Hope

44. The George, Castleton

45. The Castle, Castleton

46. Bull's Head, Castleton

47. Peaks Inn, Castleton

48. Ye Olde Nag's Head, Castleton

49. Ye Olde Cheshire Cheese, Castleton

Day Six

50. Rambler Inn, Edale

51. Old Nag's Head, Edale

Name *(as it is to appear on the certificate)* ....

Address ....

....

Date completed ....

Don't forget the SAE